# SPIRIT OF TYNESIDE

John Gibson

JOHN DONALD PUBLISHERS LTD
*EDINBURGH*

John Donald Publishers Ltd.,
138 St Stephen Street, Edinburgh EH3 5AA

ISBN 0 85976 307 2

Phototypeset by Beecee Typesetting Services
Printed in Great Britain by Bell & Bain Ltd., Glasgow

# *Acknowledgements*

I should like to thank all those who gave up their precious time in co-operating on this book: Newcastle Chronicle and Journal Ltd for the photographs, Mona Southern for checking the proofs, and Tracie Southern for her help in travelling to do the interviews.

*J.G.*

# *Contents*

# Introduction

WHAT is a Geordie? Well, I'm one. We're a proud race of people born on the banks of the Tyne — or within spitting distance of it anyway. Our heritage is our strength, we love Geordieland whether it's the industrial grime along the banks of a great river, the smell of the pitheaps or the beautiful countryside and beaches which lie within our boundaries.

Geordies, to folk not privileged to be born in God's own country, are people with funny accents: 'Aal reet, bonny lad?' we may venture when meeting a marra. 'Fancy a quick bevvy doon the club?'

To the uninitiated we are merely enquiring about a friend's health and asking if he would, perhaps, like to partake of a beverage at the local hostelry.

Geordieland has no definite boundaries. But try to tell us that someone born in Sunderland is a Geordie and you're likely to be rendered incapacitated for a few hours!

The definition of the word Geordie is lost in the mists of time. There are, of course, several explanations passed down from father to son. Really, you may take your pick.

Perhaps the most logical explanation of the word is that the coal miners of Northumberland preferred to use the safety lamp invented by George Stephenson of railway fame as opposed to the one invented by Sir Humphrey Davy. George Stephenson was employed for a time at Killingworth Colliery in Northumberland and his lamps became known colloquially by the miners as 'a Geordie', this obviously being a derivative of George.

Eventually the expression was transferred to the miners themselves. From this, so it's said, the term increased its coverage to include the whole of the industrial belt around the Tyne.

Another explanation, which is not quite so complimentary,

is that in 1826 when George Stephenson gave evidence before a Parliamentary Commission on Railways his blunt speech and dialect drew contemptuous sneers. From that date Londoners began to call the keelmen who carried the coal to the Thames 'Geordies' as a derogatory term.

A third is much simpler. Tyneside supporters of King George I were called Geordies to distinguish them from Jacobites.

So there you have it. Local historians can come up with further interpretations. It's merely a matter of choice. But like the Scousers, Cockneys or Jocks, we revel in our birthright, believing no other place in God's big world is quite like ours.

The Geordies have always thrown up great and famous people. Sportsmen, politicians, writers, adventurers, actors, men of music. . . they have all seen the first light of day on or near the banks of the Tyne.

Local songs abound, with Blaydon Races probably our national anthem, but the first line of one local ditty probably sums up the situation perfectly. 'Wherever you go you're bound to find a Geordie' has rung true for me all over the world.

In dealing with famous Geordies I've only adhered to one rule — they must still be living. And it's been more difficult curtailing the final list rather than padding it out.

Some are obvious candidates like world-famous novelist Catherine Cookson. No one has written more vividly or painted a more fascinating picture of Tyneside at the start of the century than this wonderful lady. Stories of cobbled streets, back-to-back houses with outside toilets and tin baths in front of a coal fire. Men with cloth caps and watch chains hanging from their waistcoats enjoying a pint at the end of a day of graft. Warm-hearted folk with few pennies but an indomitable spirit. . . these were the Geordies of yesteryear.

A second writer, Ian La Frenais, is another automatic choice. He may have moved on to a Los Angeles mansion and to a film and TV career which is international, but in his heart he has never left his roots. His gift is to capture the unique humour of the Geordies and transfer it brilliantly to the screen.

His first success, 'The Likely Lads', was the tale of two Geordies trying to be jack the lads while always falling somewhat short of their goal. And who can forget Oz, the character he created in 'Auf Wiedersehen Pet'? If Andy Capp had established a certain image, Oz went further. He was more of today, a lovable layabout 'as thick as a brick nettie' as we would say in these parts. La Frenais poked fun at ourselves but we loved it.

All Geordies are not Andy Capp or Oz's of course. We have produced folk who began with nowt and went on to untold fame and riches. One such man is John Hall, the son of an Ashington miner who himself started work at the pits but through sheer hard graft and vision beyond the normal became a multi-millionaire with his own aeroplane and private pilot and a stately home, Wynyard Hall, which rivals Buckingham Palace in grandeur.

John made it through property development, building the MetroCentre on bogland at Gateshead. It was the biggest indoor shopping centre in Europe, yet everyone told him his dream could never be achieved. What he did against all the odds stands as a monument for every self-made man.

Who has risen further, I might add, than Cardinal Basil Hume, the Archbishop of Westminster and leader of five million Roman Catholics in England and Wales? He began life in the Jesmond area of Newcastle as George Hume, one of five children of Sir William and Lady Hume whom his father hoped might one day become a footballer.

Men of courage as well as vision are a trademark of the area and none more so than David Scott Cowper. Born within the boundaries of Newcastle, the globe has become his canvas as he has sailed into history. A round-the-world yachtsman, David has overcome the bleak loneliness as well as mountainous seas and permanent peril to beat the records of such accomplished performers as Sir Francis Chichester, Chay Blyth and Naomi James in sailing round the world. It's little wonder that he was named in the prestigious Man of the Year awards of 1980.

Tyneside can also claim Lord Justice Peter Taylor, the son of a Gosforth doctor who was educated at Newcastle's Royal Grammar School. The Taylor Report into the Hillsborough tragedy in which 95 people died has had a far-reaching effect on football, scuppering, as it did, the Government's plans for ID cards and demanding all-seater stadia throughout the country.

Before being made a judge he earned a reputation as a brilliant advocate, appearing for the prosecution in such celebrated cases as the Jeremy Thorpe trial and the Poulson corruption hearing. He became a High Court judge in 1980 and seven years later gained his present position as one of the five new Lord Justices of Appeal approved by the Queen. Away from the bench he is Sir Peter Murray Taylor.

From an eminent judge to an eminent doctor — Miriam Stoppard, MB, BS, MD, MRCP. Married to famous playwright Tom Stoppard, she worked in clinical medicine, specialising in dermatology, and joined the pharmaceutical industry, becoming a research director. But it was TV which made Miriam a star to millions with shows such as 'Where There's Life' and a series of books on healthcare.

In the world of pop music the Geordies have also excelled. Two kids who attended Rutherford Grammar School in Newcastle took their guitars to London and became stars. Their names: Bruce Welch and Hank Marvin. Their group, The Shadows, first backed Cliff Richard and then became recognised in their own right.

Many, many more were to follow the example of Bruce and Hank. A Geordie group, The Animals, hit No. 1 with 'House of the Rising Sun' which led to one of their members, Alan Price, having a fabulous solo career. Another local band, Geordie, also made the charts with their lead singer Brian Johnson becoming a millionaire after fronting the Aussie group AC DC.

And from today's crop of new talent comes a gifted singer Neil Tennant of the Pet Shop Boys.

But towering above them all in terms of charisma and superstardom is Sting, who represents the world of pop music in this book.

Born Gordon Sumner, the son of a Wallsend milkman, he was a primary school teacher and a member of the Newcastle jazz combo, Last Exit, before joining Police and launching an international career on the back of hit upon hit record. He left the group in 1986 to pursue a solo singing and acting career which brought him back to Tyneside to film 'Stormy Monday'.

Those who tread the stage or set with words rather than

music are plentiful, too. A film star in the truest sense is Newcastle-born Bill Travers, he of 'Born Free' fame who starred with his actress wife Virginia McKenna.

The small screen of television has been blessed by Wendy Craig, a pert, bubbly actress from the small village of Sacriston who starred in such outstanding sit coms as 'And Mother Makes Three', 'Not In Front Of The Children', 'Nanny' and 'Butterflies'. Then there is comedian Jack Douglas, who took his slapstick successfully into several of the famous 'Carry On' films plus the more serious Royal Shakespearian actors John Woodvine (who also starred in TV's 'Z Cars'), and Alun Armstrong.

'Auf Wiedersehen Pet' brought to national attention three Geordie actors Jimmy Nail, Tim Healy and Kevin Whately who, as brickies first in Germany and then Spain in the follow-up series, kept us all with a wide grin on our faces.

So, too, does the inimitable Rowan Atkinson whose brilliant interpretation of Blackadder, with that marvellous rubbery face, was a natural award winner. Born at Gosforth and raised as a farmer's son in Stocksfield and Consett, he studied electrical engineering at Newcastle University before, while at Oxford on a three-year MSc course, he drifted into revue work. From there it was a short step to 'Not The Nine O'clock News' and national celebrity status.

To make great artists it takes great directors behind the camera, of course, and South Shields-born Ridley Scott has several box office hits to his credit including 'Alien', 'Bladerunner and 'Black Rain' starring Michael Douglas.

Sport is very much part of our lives in this corner of England and we have produced our own heroes. . . men who have excelled on the playing fields both nationally and internationally. Traditionally football is the greatest love of the Geordies, and standing at the very pinnacle are two brothers from the mining stock of Ashington. Bobby and Jack Charlton not only played for famous clubs — Manchester United and Leeds United — but became the first brothers to play in the same full England international side and, even more significant, on a never-to-be forgotten June day in 1966 helped England win the World Cup.

Bobby, as swift and graceful as a deer in full flight, was the artist with Jack the stopper centre-half hewn out of the black gold beneath the surface of his home town. Both have gone on to further greatness after retiring as a player — Bobby with his beloved Manchester United as a director and Jack, after successfully managing three Football League clubs including Newcastle United, taking over the Republic of Ireland international squad to lift them to previously unattained heights.

While the Charlton brothers stand out as the pair who must be featured in any book on great living Geordies, many, many others have graced the game in modern times. Such has been the quality of performance that in the last decade three local heroes who played for Newcastle United have broken the transfer record. Peter Beardsley was the first with a £1.9m transfer to Liverpool, then Paul Gascoigne whose fee was £2m, paid by Spurs, and finally Chris Waddle went to Marseille in France for £4.25m.

All played for England, of course, as did the likes of Dennis Tueart (Manchester City) and Ray Kennedy (Liverpool), while top Geordie managers have included Howard Kendall, Lawrie McMenemy, Jimmy Adamson and Bob Stokoe.

As I've already mentioned, the boundaries of Geordieland remain obscure and those on the borderline, and therefore debatable as *bona fide* Geordie passport holders, include former England manager Bobby Robson, his captain Bryan Robson and men of the calibre of Colin Bell, Colin Todd and Alan Kennedy — all England internationals.

While football dominates the back pages of the region's newspapers, other sports have produced their own men out of the ordinary. Athletics, which has blossomed at Gateshead's International Stadium, boasts Brendan Foster and Steve Cram, Olympians both. Foster was the trail blazer, a world record holder, European champion and Olympic bronze medallist at 10,000 metres. When he hung up his spikes to develop the sport as an administrator, Cram took over. With the blond looks of a Greek god and a stride as long as a pit shaft, he broke the Seb Coe and Steve Ovett domination of the classical 1,500 metres to become World, European and Commonwealth champion and an Olympic silver medallist in Los Angeles.

Mike McLeod, from the Elswick district of Newcastle, also deserves a mention with his silver medal in the Olympic 10,000 metres of 1984 standing as the highlight of a long and distinguished career.

Professional boxing, so often weaned in the working-class atmosphere of a big city, was the relief of many a working man during the hungry years of the 20's and 30's and in 1989 Tyneside at last gave us a world champion in Glenn McCrory, who took the International Boxing Federation version of the world cruiser-weight title.

McCrory represents the more acceptable face of boxing. Clean cut with the handsome looks of a male model, there isn't a cauliflower ear or broken nose in sight. Considerate and without a trace of arrogance, he adheres strictly to his Catholic upbringing. A thoroughly nice and placid man in a violent world.

Cricket, so much more genteel and sedate with thoughts of cucumber sandwiches eaten in a deckchair on a balmy sunny day, hasn't seen the first-class game reach such northern boundaries as yet but that hasn't stopped men of the Tyne going south in search of fame if not fortune. Perhaps the most colourful and biggest crowd pleaser has been Burnopfield's Colin Milburn, a roly poly batsman with Northants and England who would smite the ball a mile as though swatting an irritating fly.

Ollie became a good mate and when he died suddenly during the writing of this book it was a massive blow to all of us. A shaft of light had been switched off forever. He was a raconteur with a fund of funny stories gathered from around the world who regaled many a crowd on a wet day when rain had stopped play, propped up against the bar with his favourite pint in his hand. His playing career had been cruelly cut short when he lost an eye in a car accident, but though he returned to his roots to live he wasn't lost totally to cricket. He took his wit and his shrewd assessment of the game into the BBC radio commentary box at Test matches and was also a noted after-dinner speaker.

There have been, and still are, other cricketing stars originating from our boundaries. For example, what about Tom Graveney, as graceful a strokemaker as you're likely to find who played in 79 Tests for England?

Oh, he's ours right enough. His father was a manager at Vickers Armstrong at their Elswick works in the west end of Newcastle and Tom was born in the Northumbrian village of Riding Mill from where his mother also came. His grandfather and grandmother ran the local pub in the village, the Railway Inn, and in his formative years young Graveney also lived first in Jesmond and then Fenham. The back of the house in Moorside North looked out onto the Town Moor, where Tom first learned to hold a cricket bat after his father had cut a hole in the hedge for easy access.

But I'm reluctant to include Graveney as a Geordie Great. Not because of any possible flaw in a cricketing giant — good gracious no — but simply because he left the area 'at about seven or eight'.

Geordie-born, yes, but a genuine Geordie star? Maybe not. It would be even harder to lay claim to Harry Patterson, who under the alias Jack Higgins became one of our most prolific thriller writers. Again, he was born locally in Elswick on July 27, 1929, the son of a Tyneside shipyard worker. But after only a year he departed for Belfast and then, at the age of 11, found himself in Leeds.

It's worked the other way, too, of course. The 'foreigner' who moved to Tyneside at an early age and grew up as one of us. Mark Knofler, the front man of that phenomenally successful group Dire Straits, was born in Glasgow but is regularly — and wrongly — referred to as a Geordie because he was raised in Gosforth.

But enough of the maybes. Let's instead return to the genuine article — and it must be said that the ladies have also made a considerable contribution to our sporting heritage. Karen Straker, a Newcastle-born horsewoman of international standing, was in Britain's 1988 Olympic three-day eventing team, along with Mark Phillips, which won the silver medal, while Crawcrook's Diane Bell is the Olympic and former world judo champion at under 61 kg.

Then there is Joanne Conway, the four-times British figure-skating champion who first took the title at the age of 14 — the youngest title-winner for 32 years.

## Introduction

Beauty as well as athletic prowess is a feature of Geordie lasses. Madeleine Stringer became Miss UK and married local lad Chas Chandler, who played with The Animals and went on to manage groups such as Slade, while Pat Morgan was Miss Great Britain and now runs a successful model agency in Newcastle.

So there we are . . . famous people from a famous area. People who have enhanced our everyday lives. Northern folk with a great passion and commitment which will be carried on forever.

Perhaps the feeling of so many Geordies was best summed up by Jackie Milburn, a footballing legend who was the epitome of Tyneside at its very best. Warm, caring and successful.

Wor Jackie once told me: 'I never feel better than when I'm crossing the Tyne Bridge and can smell the pitheaps. That's when I know I'm home.'

# Catherine Cookson

IN 1950, and at the age of 44, she had her first novel published. Yet today, Catherine Cookson O.B.E. is world-famous, avidly read by millions across the earth in seventeen different languages. A lady of rare, rich talent — the world's favourite story teller.

What makes her quite remarkable is that her own life is as fascinating, as heartrending and as tragic as any piece of fiction. Born eighty-four years ago into abject poverty in Tyne Dock, next door to a pub known as '27', Katie McMullen grew up in a three-roomed flat at 10 William Black Street, East Jarrow. Illegitimate, she was taunted by playmates telling her: 'Ye've got no da',' and emotionally scarred by her mother Kate's alcoholism.

She spent 14½ years in the laundries of various work-houses, ten of those years as manageress. But if the early years of her life were exceptionally hard, the middle ones were the most unhappy. As she herself says; 'I now look back on the years between the ages of 45 and 60 as a painful nightmare,' for these were the years in which she was fighting the breakdown that had hit her in 1945: the loss of her first baby was followed by three miscarriages. And yet, extraordinarily it was during these years she wrote what are probably her best stories; and two of them were made into films by J. Arthur Rank at Pinewood as 'Jacqueline' and 'Rooney'.

When, in her teens, she began to bleed profusely she had no idea that she was suffering from a vascular disease assuredly passed on from her unknown father, who, she had been given to understand by her aunt, was a gentleman, a fact she admits she held on to, for she was convinced she had inherited qualities that could never have come from Kate. Yet she also admits life has taught her that what she did inherit from her mother, such as a sense of humour and kindness of heart, are of more value in the long run than her talents. Even so, it is this gift that has become her prop, her driving force, her reason to live (husband Tom apart).

After writing her first sixteen books in longhand — an awesome task — she got writer's cramp and thought her writing days were over. But when Tom suggested she use a tape recorder a new area opened for her. Being a natural talker the stories just flowed out. But, Catherine stresses, the talking is only the beginning, for after the words are taken down off the machine, the hard work begins, and during the following weeks she will correct her story at least three times, polishing it like a precious diamond, and then only, will she let Tom look at it. Eventually when what should be the final copy is typed ready for the publisher, she will go over her work again, which often results in more deleting and anything from thirty to fifty pages to be re-typed.

And this she accomplishes in spite of being confined to bed for long periods because of her inherited blood trouble, which is no respecter of either time or of place.

'I can never understand,' she said, 'when people say they haven't an idea in their head and can sit staring at a blank page waiting for inspiration. But then I'm very fortunate, I'm never stuck for an idea: in between checking one story I can be talking down another.'

She has had more than eighty books published, her publisher has another six awaiting their turn, and she has four at home which she's polishing up . . . 'between times,' she laughs.

Mrs Cookson may have spent more than forty-five years 'in exile' in the south but her prolific output of millions of words has seen her rarely stray from the topic she knows best — the people of the North East, their surroundings, their experiences, hopes and dreams.

'All my books bar two,' she says, 'have been set in this area. At one time I would have questioned the possibility of writing eighty books with similar backgrounds and still maintain their readers' interest, but then it's people who make the story and human nature is the same the world over. And whether one wants to believe it or not, class distinctions are as alive in the north as they are in the south.

'I am dubbed,' she says, 'merely a writer of the working class. This is a misconception, as any critic who has really read my books will concede: all my work touches on the class structure of both the working and the middle class for I am conversant with both.

'I started writing at eleven,' she told me in one of her rare interviews these days. 'But I must have been about sixteen when, full of hope, I sent my first short story to the *Shields Gazette*. I posted it on a Wednesday, they received it on the Thursday, and I got it back on the Friday! Many years later I met the man who must have thrown my very amateurish manuscript back at the postman and we had a laugh about it. But I recall that, at the time, I bubbled, while me granda poured his vehement sympathy over me, saying: "Never you mind, hinny. What do they know about writin' that lot in Tyne Dock office? Why, they're nowt but a lot of dozy . . . budgerigars." Or words to that effect!

'I recall, too, that when I was much younger, he had warned me that my "spinning yarns" to anyone who would listen would eventually get me into either the clink or into the money.

'Like many Northerners,' she went on, 'I thought I knew it all by the time I was twenty. Yet at least, by that time I was sure of what I wanted to be. And that was a lady, one who talked proper . . . God help me!'

She was laughing here. 'It wasn't until, by mere chance, while reading a book by Elinor Glynn, that I came across the name of Lord Chesterfield. A character in the book was advising the heroine that if she wanted to be educated she must begin to read the Earl's letters. Without further to do I dashed down to the South Shields library and got out the first volume of Lord Chesterfield's *Letters To His Son*. It was at this point I can truthfully say my life changed. The writings of this man pointed out very forcibly my abysmal ignorance. I hadn't read a book of any import, and I had been nowhere except on a flying visit to Ireland. My first efforts towards culture, however, were to end in failure. I tried to learn to play the violin and to speak French. In the first instance there must have been something wrong with the fiddle, for very soon it became evident I couldn't play it. In the latter effort my failure was due to the teacher, oh undoubtedly, for she couldn't get my accent right, no more than she could her own.

'But here I was with my eyes being opened to myself, and realising for the first time what this gnawing inside me was all about. So from then on this man Philip Dormer Stanhope, 4th Earl of Chesterfield, became my tutor, and the public library my university. Through him I read my first real history and geography, I was introduced to mythology; but most of all I was gradually led to read the great writers of the past, Chaucer, John Donne, Pope, Voltaire, Dean Swift to name but a few.

'I can't claim to have studied these writers, at first it was a readers' digest effort. But over the following ten years, during which I worked never less than twelve hours a day, and much of it manual work, and I mean manual work, which included mixing cement to lay paths around the house, and digging drains after a day in the laundry I would, at times, burn the midnight oil in order to keep in touch with my dear Lord Chesterfield. But what I found more wearing on my already depleted system was the mental stress as my mother was once again in my life.'

This way of life continued until she met Tom, a grammar school master, and at this point her life changed again. But they were not married until June 1, 1940 and a month later they were evacuated to St. Albans.

'And,' she says, 'for the first time in my life I experienced supreme happiness, and time to read . . . and sleep, wonderful sleep, for from the beginning of the war I'd had twelve blind men from the East End of London billeted on me, some were ailing, one was bedridden. I cooked for them, washed their anything but pleasant clothes — no washing machine, I stamped them out in the bath — even had the awkward job of shaving the bedridden eighty-year-old. I had one young girl helper. Looking back I know I was only kept going at that time by Tom's practical help after school, and his unfailing and patient love.'

It was hardly surprising that, with her crippling early life, Catherine turned away from the Catholic church, and her voice was firm as she said: 'No; I don't believe in the God put over by denominations, but I do believe that we are part of a spiritual being, and I accept the parable of Jesus when He said, "The kingdom of God is within you." I believe it is: we only have to recognise it.'

Though not religious, Catherine is a highly moral person. 'I don't write about blatant sex,' she says with a pride in the knowledge that her books still sell in their millions without the need for titillation.

She has strong views about many things; and drunkenness, which used to be termed the prerogative of the working classes, is something else she abhors after an upbringing surrounded by it. When a local pub tried to use her name to drum up business Mrs Cookson firmly killed the idea.

*Our Kate,* her autobiography, is a touching and rather gentle book, which first appeared in 1968. But even now, twenty-two years on, people still write to her saying what a profound effect it has had on their lives. As she says: 'I knew I couldn't write about my mother until after she had died, which happened in 1956. The first script was so filled with bitterness I knew I could never let it go as it stood, although I knew the bitterness to be justified, and during the following twelve years I rewrote it no less than eight times.

'Even then, I was in two minds about letting it be published, and when it finally came out the reactions to it were surprising, at least one of them was.

'I had never been worried about reactions to my books, because they were mostly favourable, but my autobiography was a new baby, and I waited for the telephone to ring. When it did, the voices of two so-called friends, who lived in St Leonards and who were originally from the north, vied with each other in saying, "Oh dear," and "Oh, my dear, what have you done? We have just read the book and we think you've made a great mistake. Oh, my dear, you should never have done it. You have lost your image, dear, for, you know, up till now you could have been taken for a lady." '

Her early ambition was, as she said, to aspire to be a lady, and she now admits her aim then was to fit herself to step into her father's world, when she should find him. And so, during her teens she did search for him but to no avail; she says if Kate had known what she was up to she would have murdered her.

Her mail is enormous — at one time it was three thousand letters a year. She doesn't know what it is now, only that she is finding difficulty in answering it, and since she has been so ill of late, Tom has had to take it on completely. She always said she would never reply to a letter by secretary notes, or photostat letters, but of late she has been forced to, especially with the spate of charity appeals and begging letters of all kinds. Here, she says wistfully: 'These have really got out of hand. People don't realise that I am not a company or corporation, I am just a single person, and that I have to keep writing to bring money in.'

Yet I see her as many others do, for a whole new industry has grown up around South Tyneside, renamed in 1984 Catherine Cookson Country at a time when the area was taking an economic battering with yard, shop and factory closures at every turn. While the politicians struggled to get help from the Government, they also set to work to tackle their own problems at local level.

Tourism appeared to be the answer but cash was tight. Seafront schemes met hostile opposition from locals, and tour operators around the country weren't exactly lining up to bring coach visitors to South Shields. So what was their greatest asset? The answer was obvious: Catherine Cookson.

Though she prefers to be out of the limelight, living quietly with her work, she still treasures the unbreakable link with her fans. 'The best thing,' she says, 'is when I get a letter which begins: "I'd never read a book in my life until I got one of yours, and now I can't stop." And these come from women in their middle years. I always reply: "Read everything you can get your hands on, and a new world will open up for you." '

Her other great source of comfort, pride and love is husband Tom. On June 1, 1990, they celebrated fifty years of happy marriage, nineteen days before her eighty-fourth birthday. The devotion and the caring is still there, perhaps stronger than ever. 'He is,' she says without a hint of slushiness, 'the man who was made for me. He is everything I could ever want — the kindest, most caring person in the world and compensation for anything I have ever suffered.'

When at the age of fifty-seven he had to retire from teaching through severe migraine which had plagued him for years, he, the mathematician and Oxford graduate — and the keen footballer, cricketer and boxer — was prepared to take on the cooking and the housework so that she could concentrate on her writing.

Tom's devotion is summed up in her own words. 'He was prepared, without so much as a second thought, to do what most husbands, especially in the scholastic world, would find desperately difficult, that is change roles. But not only that, he continued to be my critic and adviser. This I may confess did not run as smoothly all the time as did his cooking and his polishing, for he is a very finicky critic.'

When in 1976 they returned to the north, after forty-six years in Hastings, it had been, she confesses, not her idea but his. For what he said to her was: 'You should die among your ain folk.' She recalls: 'I was only seventy at the time. Of course it was only an excuse for he was ready for a change; and what was more, he had taken a liking for Newcastle whilst on our visits back here — not to mention the people.

'Candidly, I didn't want to move. We had a beautiful home, with an indoor swimming pool and a most lovely garden that had taken us twenty-two years to make, during which time Tom had become very knowledgeable about Rhododendrons and Azaleas. Nevertheless, we moved, and although for the first year I was homesick, not so much for the house, but for my garden, I know now it was the right thing to do. If for nothing else, for the wonderful medical treatment I have received and the friends I have made, not forgetting the love that has openly flowed to me from the northerners themselves.'

Naturally such a phenomenally successful writer has been honoured many times over.

The first came from South Shields. She says: 'Writers are rarely given the freedom of boroughs. So I was indeed very surprised and pleased when the council approached me. They were first to recognise me; they didn't wait until I was dead — it's hard to appreciate honours from the grave.'

Catherine's M.A. from Newcastle University was, indeed, something else. 'I've always regretted not having had a university education and so I was delighted to enter, even if it was through the back door.'

Mrs Cookson was also the subject of the 'This Is Your Life' programme, and was named a Paul Harris Fellow by the Rotary International.

What has pleased her too, and she considers it an honour, was being invited separately by the Union Societies of Cambridge and Oxford to be the guest of honour at dinner and afterwards to address the Union. She would have loved to accept these invitations, but they came at times when, unfortunately, she was too ill to travel. She admits she loved giving talks, and for the first twenty years of her career she frequently did what she calls her platform stunts, never missing a chance to put over her dear Lord Chesterfield.

But without a doubt, her O.B.E. must rank above everything else. Especially as it brought her such a special meeting with the Prince of Wales.

'I wasn't able to go to London to receive my honour from the Queen because of health problems, but when the Prince of Wales came to Shields he presented the medal to me in private, in a room set apart with Tom, my specialist and his wife, and my secretary and her husband, plus the Prince and his own TV crew.

'In order not to be disappointed this second time, I got out of bed, where I'd been for some weeks, to keep this wonderful appointment. We had a police escort from my front door all the way to Shields. But imagine my feelings when they had to stop the cars so that I could get out and be sick! Can you believe it? When we arrived at the hall I had fifteen minutes in which to pull myself together.

'The Prince spent twenty minutes with me, and we laughed and talked. It was simply wonderful. He's a marvellous man. It was a day never to be forgotten.

'Towards the end of his stay, which was two hours later, everyone was lined up in the hall, and I understand the Prince, on his way to the door, looked over towards my little group, then stopped before walking across to my specialist and saying: 'How is Mrs Cookson?'

'Not very well, Sir,' Mr Marshall replied.

'Oh, I am so sorry,' he said.

'With everything on his mind, and nearly two hours after meeting me, he was concerned enough to inquire about my health. It was a wonderful gesture. Later in the year, a book came out dealing with twelve months in his life, and I was honoured to find part of our conversation was in it. I think the Prince is marvellous. There are two men in my life; Tom and Charles. I adore them both!'

No one could spend time with Catherine Cookson and fail to ask two questions every single reader must yearn to ask: what is her favourite book and has she, after all these years, any ambitions left?

To the first she replies without a moment's hesitation: 'My favourite book is the next one. If I was utterly satisfied with my latest effort, I'd give up. I keep telling myself that one day I'll write a really good book!'

Of her ambition, she says thoughtfully: 'My first wish is utterly impossible — to have good health. But after that, the only thing I want is peace of mind and spiritual awareness. But please, may I say I don't wish, as has happened in the past, for a spate of letters telling me this can so easily be achieved!'

I'm sure her millions of readers across the world will be with her in all she wishes for herself. For someone who gives so much pleasure deserves a little of her own.

# Sting

HIS face was the face of the eighties . . . handsome, even beautiful, gaunt, fine-boned and undeniably sexy. His distinctive voice, unique ability as a composer, and natural charisma made him a pop sensation. Out of the punk era of the middle and late seventies came The Police, a group he didn't form but fronted and eventually devoured with his own personality.

But whereas the Sex Pistols were too abrasive, too revolting, for a mass market, The Police — and Sting — adopted a much more musical approach. They added a touch of reggae and a stamp of their own. They were articulate, intellectual and, in a very short space of time, millionaires. Hits flowed . . . No. 1's like 'Message in a Bottle', 'Walking on the Moon', 'Don't Stand so Close to Me', 'Every Little Thing She Does is Magic', and 'Every Breath You Take'.

Sting was what he always knew he would be. A superstar. A solo career followed after he left the group in 1986 and a career as a film star. It was the classic pop story — the boy from the city who made it all the way to the top.

Sting was born Gordon Sumner, the son of a Wallsend milkman and a hairdresser. The year was 1951 and the North East, like so many big industrial towns, was trying to recover from a world war. He lived in Station Road, Wallsend and helped deliver milk from his father's dairy opposite St. Luke's.

It was a background which in later life didn't hold any particular appeal to the young man with a new name. Unlike most Geordies who gained either fame or fortune — or both in his case — he neither clung to his roots nor looked back on Newcastle with great affection. Not for him what he saw as the falseness of those who left the place as fast as they could and then eulogised about it.

Journalist Phil Sutcliffe, with whom I used to work and who wrote the official biography of The Police, recalled Sting telling him: 'Saying Newcastle is a great place, I can't stand that. Newcastle's a **** place. It was a slum from the industrial revolution and when they knocked down the old slums they built new slums.

'I don't want to be rooted in Newcastle. I don't want to be a Geordie. I've got none of that awful pride.'

Sting's untold riches have come from simply 'doing what he wanted to do', says Sutcliffe. And what hurts him still is that the world — and perhaps Tyneside in particular — is full of people who are prevented from doing what they want to do.

Sting was, of course, and still is, different. A paradox, someone who freely admits he doesn't quite know what he is going to say or do next. A man who is either 'a raving loony or in the depths of despair.'

He is a walking contradicition — a Socialist who has pots of money. He is also a realist and a champion of causes. A megastar who fits comfortably into what that means. And, whether he likes it or not, definitely a Geordie!

The eldest of four children born to Audrey and Ernie Sumner (the others are brother Philip and sisters Angela and Anita), he first attended St Columba's First School in Wallsend and when he passed his eleven plus moved on to St. Cuthbert's Grammar School in the city. But passing the exam also marked a significant development in his love of music.

Ernie, who sadly died shortly after Audrey in 1987, said: 'Shortly before his eleven plus a friend of mine gave Gordon an old guitar. He was really keen on it and used to sit and strum away on it for hours. I told him that if he passed the exam he could have a bicycle or a guitar. He wasn't interested in the bike like other youngsters, just a new guitar.'

His father bought him a £15 guitar — 'something that I could ill afford at the time' — and Gordon never looked back.

'With one hand he would play the guitar and with the other he would do his homework. And he would be watching television at the same time!

'I sent Gordon to a guitar teacher in Walkerville but only

weeks later the man phoned me up to say that Gordon was wasting his time and my money. Gordon didn't want to be taught. He wanted to learn everything himself.'

School friends and teachers alike remember the young Sting as a quiet lad who played rugby for the school and was an outstanding athlete. Nothing too unusual.

'I read later that Gordon was supposed to be a rebel,' said Dave Stapylton, a classmate in the late sixties who is now back at St. Cuthbert's as head of the middle school. 'That made me laugh. It was so much rubbish but I suppose it was the right image for a rock and roll star. In fact he was a quiet, sensitive boy, not a bit coarse. He had quite a refined voice — not a trace of a Geordie accent like some of the lads. When I see him interviewed on telly now he sounds exactly the same as he did at school.'

By the third year Stapylton and Sumner were in the same class and travelled daily to school together.

'I got on the train at Howdon and he got on at Wallsend further down the line,' Dave told me. 'We used to leave it as late as possible. I caught the train at 8.39, he got on at Wallsend at 8.42 and the trrain arrived at the Central Station in Newcastle at 8.59 a.m. Then it was a chase to catch the bus to the west end of the city — if we missed it we were late for school. Gordon was a great sprinter, good enough to run for the county, so I let him set off like the wind and he held onto the bus until I got there!'

Like most 14-year-olds Gordon would join in pranks aimed at taking the micky out of the schoolmasters.

'We both went on a school holiday to Loch Ailort in the Scottish Highlands near Fort William,' recalled Dave. 'The commandoes had used it as their training ground during the war and we stayed in the nissen huts which had been their barracks. It was perfect for kids — run down and a place where you could make as much noise as you liked. We had the usual pillow fights and all that.

'One day one of the staff had left his car open in front of the huts. Gordon, myself and a few of the other lads took the handbrake off and pushed it round the back out of view. When the teacher surfaced he thought his car had been pinched. There was a right commotion. We were on jankers for a while after that.'

Even at that early stage Sting was a hit with the girls, long before his newly acquired blond looks on stage sent thousands of hearts fluttering.

'It rained all week and our clothes were soaked by the time we set off home. We caught the train to Mallaig, a fishing port, and spent half an hour there before moving on to Fort William. While we were in Mallaig two girls latched onto Gordon. He wore a PVC raincoat, which was all the rage at the time, and looked dead modern. They came with us on the train to Fort William where we all went to see *The Great St. Trinians Train Robbery* at the pictures.

'Both the girls sat with Gordon. He was a bit embarrassed but dead chuffed that he had scored. The rest of us were envious. There were only two girls and Gordon had them both. They got off the train at Corpach, the first station on the journey home. I've often wondered since if they realise the young lad in the raincoat was Sting.'

Gordon's nickname at school was Noddy. 'It came about because his name spelled backwards was Nodrog Renmus and that got shortened to Noddy.' A few years later when Sting, by now the lead singer with The Police, returned to Newcastle to present the Duke of Edinburgh awards, his old PE teacher Tony Knox was telling him in the car from the airport that the *Evening Chronicle* were carrying a story about his nickname. He was so interested he insisted on stopping the car and buying six copies of the newspaper.

Music, naturally, was a major influence on the young Gordon Sumner. He often took his guitar to school and would hang out at the Duke of York in Wallsend where they held a folk club.

'Gordon was into folk music — he loved the likes of Bob Dylan,' recalls Stapylton. 'Another of his favourite groups was the Kinks. In fact he had all the mannerisms of Ray Davies, their lead singer.'

Ironically, for a school with a sound academic background and a history for producing good football sides, it's in the world of pop music that they have produced their most famous sons. Apart from Sting, Neil Tennant of the Pet Shop Boys and Ray Laidlaw of Lindisfarne are both ex-pupils.

The academic success of St. Cutherbert's is best reflected by Paul Kennedy, a Wallsend lad born in 1945 who is now professor of history at Yale University in America.

But initially it was in the world of sport that Gordon excelled. He was an outstanding sprinter over 100 and 220 yards, a fair long jumper and played rugby for the school using his pace on the wing.

'But it was the football team which won all the attention,' Stapylton told me. 'I played football rather than rugby and we won the All England Cup.

'The rugby team was struggling when we were in the fourth year and they arranged matches at a different time to the soccer games so that a few of the football players could help out. One day we were playing Heaton Grammar School at rugby and Hughie McBride, our skipper, switched over from football. He didn't know a thing about rugby and was appealing to the referee for obstruction. Gordon had to take him to one side and explain the rules.'

McBride, now a schoolmaster at Heaton Manor in the city, turned up later at a Police concert in America, knocked on the stage door, and asked for Sting. He watched the concert as Sting's guest, went back with him to the group's hotel, and drank the night away on champagne!

PE teacher Tony Knox remembers Sumner with affection. 'He was a natural sprinter, someone with unbelievable ability. All the top sprinters have the knack of looking relaxed when they perform and so had Gordon. I was always onto him. "You're not trying, lad," I would say. He had a clipped style of running and looked to be putting in no effort.

'But he was the Northumberland and Durham sprint champion and at the inter-county meeting on a cinder track at Houghton he took that title as well. He went on to run at the national championships which is quite something.

'He was the sort of lad who would have a bash at anything and took part in the long jump and triple jump. His natural pace made him a fair rugby player but he was a gentle person. He wasn't aggressive in any way like a lot of rugby players.'

Knox, who played left-back for England's amateur side and

made two Amateur Cup semi-final appearances with Whitley Bay, was the person behind Sting's visit to the city to present the Duke of Edinburgh awards shortly after fame had beckoned.

'I was in charge of the scheme at the time and he agreed to come back to the Civic Centre in Newcastle for the presentation. He did it all for nothing — no expenses or hotel or anything like that. I know he could afford it but it was a nice gesture all the same. And he took it ever so seriously. He wrote to me asking about the award scheme and its aims and produced a magnificent speech.

'Gordon always had strong political beliefs — Socialism was his thing and a passionate belief in equality of opportunity.

'When I met him at the airport he had a bodyguard and all the trimmings of a pop star. But he was the same lad I remembered. He was wearing his old St. Cuthebert's school tie — he told me he rarely wore a tie but had put one on just for me — and popped over to have a chat with his sister who was working at one of the check-outs at the airport before travelling into the city. I was impressed by the way he handled his fame.'

That ability to cast aside the nonsense which can be written about pop stars in some of the more lurid newspapers is something which became a necessary part of Sting's make-up as fame became even more worldwide.

'We talked about some reports that he used to be caned at school. The headmaster was a priest and he had been upset to read such things. It was just a small point but Sting explained that items like that — wrongly attributed to him — arose all the time. "I can't sue everyone or I'd be in court all the time," he said and, of course, he was right.'

For Sting, progression meant teacher-training college and then a job teaching at St. Paul's RC First School in Doddington Drive, Cramlington. 'I did teaching well, very well. I learnt to entertain delinquents for an hour. Same as now. I learnt timing, rapport, how to talk to kids without making them think you're a jerk. The trouble was a lot of them had never really been talked with.'

But all the time music was very much part of his life. Father Duffy from his old school, St. Cuthbert's, recalls going to the

University Theatre in Newcastle to see *Joseph and His Amazing Technicolour Dreamcoat,* and there was Gordon Sumner in the backing group.

His new name, which was to kill stone dead Gordon Sumner forever, came about in 1975 when he used to play in a combo called The Phoenix Jazz Men, wearing a black and yellow striped jumper. 'The trombone player called me Sting. I liked the name and it stuck.'

After the Phoenix Jazz Men Sting spent time in the Newcastle Big Band before joining a jazz rock group, Last Exit, who played regularly at places like the Gosforth Hotel.

'We got to be the biggest thing in Newcastle and decided to move to London. But after I'd moved down the other guys decided that they couldn't leave their secure jobs back home. So I was left in London alone and starving — literally — when Stewart Copeland, who used to be the drummer with Curved Air, asked me to join his new band Police. I was in two bands at the same time but Last Exit was split geographically and I found it impossible to travel back to Newcastle for gigs. I preferred to be a small fish in a big pond than a big fish in a small pond.'

Sting was to become the biggest fish possible in an extremely big pond, of course. Together with Copeland and Andy Summers, who played guitar, The Police were to become a phenomenon, firstly in America and then back home.

'I used to be in Dixieland bands. Last Exit was a transition but The Police was the first out-and-out rock band I'd played in. After a while I began to write songs in the style of the band and took over the role.

'It was the end of 1976 and the whole punk thing was happening. I was a bit wary about it but I liked the aggression it brought. We tagged along with the new wave but added a more musical touch. America was also ready for the new wave but bands like the Sex Pistols were too abrasive for the US market. They needed something more musical like us and Dire Straits (their lead singer, Mark Knopfler, was also brought up in Newcastle from the age of six though he was born in Glasgow).

'I was heavily influenced by reggae ever since Bob Marley turned me on. I lived in Bayswater so it wasn't hard to hear reggae, but while there was a feeling of it our musical style was very much our own.'

Sting had met and married actress Frances Tomelty who claimed she nagged him, guided him and pushed him towards success as he lived on the floor of a friend's flat in London. In those days, she said, 'he was naive.

'He took his usual attitude of not being interested in anything but singing and playing.' It was left to her to hawk tapes of Sting's early work around the record companies. At the time Sting, already a father, was on the dole and he wrote in his diary that it was 'depressing and demeaning. It gives me nausea. I'm racked with guilt. What we are doing is either heroic or stupid. No money, nowhere to live, and neither of us has a job. Could this be the end?'

Within two years the release of the hit single 'Roxanne' and The Police's first album meant Sting could write: 'This is as far as I've ever got. The deep pile carpets, the cane furniture and the Parker Pen.'

Ironically when 'Roxanne' first came out the BBC wouldn't play it because it was about a prostitute. But when it was a huge hit in America and the US wasn't morally ruined by it, they started giving it massive air play.

Sting was officially a superstar . . . and the pop band-wagon began to roll. More hits, including No. 1's, best group in the 1980 British Rock and Pop Awards, a worldwide tour taking in places like America, Japan, Australia, Egypt, Thailand and India. It was all go and living out of a suitcase for a singer who originally dyed his hair blond for a television commercial.

But he never pretended to be the tearaway he knew he wasn't and was anxious not to be seen conforming to the head-banging stereotype. Paul Scott's *Raj Quartet*, Le Carre's *Smiley's People* and *V* by Thomas Pynchon were his light reading on tour and he would be as happy to contrast and compare the poetry of Ted Hughes and Philip Larkin as he was to discuss the relative merits of David Bowie and Paul McCartney (one of his early heroes).

The Police were the band of the early eighties until they split in '86 with Sting, like so many front men before and since, branching out into a solo career. Hit records came with the likes of 'Spread A Little Happiness', 'Russians', 'Moon over Bourbon Street' and 'An Englishman In New York' as well as LP's 'Dream Of The Blue Turtles' and 'Nothing Like The Sun', though never quite with the same mass sales as before.

The Geordie had always had acting as a second string to his bow, starring originally in The Who's film *Quadrophenia* and, while once declaring that he didn't want to be caught between two careers like David Essex, the fantasy of the screen grew more appealing.

'I made two movies before anyone knew I was a singer. I enjoy learning and challenging myself although I think I'm a more intuitive musician than I am an actor. If I can act it's because I can intellectualize what I'm trying to do — tell a story. I like characters who are complex or who have the potential to be complicated.'

Sting learned his profession alongside Meryl Streep, Denholm Elliott and Lord Olivier's wife Joan Plowright and came back to Tyneside in 1987 to film and star in *Stormy Monday*, playing a jazz club owner Mr Finney which took him back to his roots in the city.

Ironically the script was sent to him in Malibu by his Hollywood agent with the query, had he ever heard of Newcastle? 'I'm from Newcastle, you ****', he retorted and found he had known writer-director Mike Figgis back in Newcastle when Figgis played trumpet in Bryan Ferry's band The Gas Board.

'What I found surprising is how photographic Newcastle is, particularly the old parts. I hate the new parts but on the Quayside the buildings are really wonderful.'

His old master Tony Knox had described Sting to me as 'a caring, thoughtful person aware of problems of the world.' That manifested itself in his work. He did a world tour for Amnesty International with Peter Gabriel and Bruce Springstein and in Budapest, waving a copy of the Universal Declaration of Human Rights, declared: 'People in Rumania are being repressed as a minority' a full year before the bloody uprising changed the history of that country.

By 1989 Sting was campaigning vigorously to save the Amazon rain forests. He had audiences with Brazilian president

José Sarney, French president Francois Mitterrand, King Juan Carlos and Queen Sofia of Spain and even the Pope in trying to enlist support at the highest level.

The milkman's son from Wallsend has indeed come a long way.

# Bobby and Jack Charlton

**FOOTBALL** is a national pastime in England, nowhere more so than in Geordieland. Here it was said that if you shouted down a pit shaft a centre-forward would come up. The game has been revered for over a century from the days when players wore long shorts, shoe-laces in their shirts and boots which were heavy enough to give you a hernia. The traditional sport of the working class, the home of Newcastle United at St. James's Park became a shrine and the area produced an abundance of raw, exciting talent.

Perhaps the greatest family to come from the North East was the Milburn Clan of Ashington. For them, as for countless more, football was a way of life. The difference was they produced sons with exceptional gifted ability who were to light up the Football League. The family tree goes back to 1888 when Jack Milburn played in goal for Northumberland. His son, another Jack Milburn, was a tough-as-old-boots full-back with Ashington and Morpeth who became known locally as Old Warhorse. He had six sons, all of whom were noted footballers in the area. One, Alec, was the father of Jackie Milburn — the legendary Wor Jackie, who won the F.A. Cup three times with Newcastle United and went on to play for England. Another, Tanner, had four sons who all became full-backs with League clubs — Jack, George and Jimmy at Leeds United and Stan at Chesterfield. Their sister, Cissie, was later to produce two sons of her own named Bobby and Jack Charlton. Perhaps the most spectacularly successful of all the Milburn Clan.

The Charltons were to make soccer history . . . the first

brothers to play for England together and team-mates on the only occasion England have ever won the World Cup.

Cissie, who was actually christened Elizabeth but was known to all her famous brothers as Cis, spent the summer as a child training on Newbiggin beach with Jack, George, Jim and Stan 'cursing a thousand times over that I was born a lass.' Not for her dolls and prams, more footballs and marbles.

She met and married Bob Charlton, a miner at Linton Colliery whose sporting love was boxing not football. The day Bob took on the fairground pug at Paddy's Market he got knocked out in the second round but was paid a pound for his troubles. With it he bought Cissie a wedding ring for 17s 6d and they moved into Laburnum Terrace, a typical row of pit houses in Ashington, and eventually produced four sons though, unfairly, Gordon and Tommy were to be completely overshadowed outside the family home by Jack and Bobby.

They grew up during the years when Wor Jackie was king, a swashbuckling, blisteringly fast centre-forward with a shot like the kick of a mule. Bobby recalls he and Wor Jack going to the local pictures to see the newsreel of Jackie Milburn's first international match for England against Ireland. 'We were late and had to sit through Moira Shearer in *The Red Shoes* until the newsreel was repeated.'

Jack also remembers the trips to 'the toon' to watch Jackie and United.

'He was our famous uncle. Me and our kid would watch him every other Saturday at St. James's Park,' he told me. 'It was a ritual when I was around 10 or 11. Cissie would give us 2s 6d and we'd catch the bus from Ashington to the Haymarket and nick round the corner to the British Home Restaurant for our dinner. We'd grab a plate apiece and they'd serve us as we went along the line. Then we'd run up to the ground and into the popular side. We always sat at the front as near to the halfway line as possible.

'It was lovely watching Jackie, Joe Harvey, Bobby Cowell and the rest. We could see stars.

'After the game we'd go across the road and queue to get into St. James's Hall and watch the wrestling. That finished around 9.30 p.m. and we'd catch the last bus to Ashington where either my mother or father was waiting at the bus stop to take us home.'

Actually Cissie had introduced the boys to football at a much earlier age.

'I took Jack and Bobby with me to Ashington's home games from a very early age. Poor little Bobby, just a babe in his pram, would jump with fright at the roar whenever a goal was scored.'

Though brothers with strikingly similar features — both now have thin whispy hair covering their domes — they were, and still are, very different in nature and attitudes. Jack was the mixer full of life and go like his mother. Bobby was shy to the point of appearing big-headed.

'Bobby was a pain in the backside to me as a kid,' said Jack with a grin as wide as the Tyne. 'He's two-and-a-half years younger than me and was a mother's boy. I had to take him with me wherever I went. I wanted to be off bird nesting and blackberrying but my mother would say: "Take our Bobby — and look after him." I didn't like that.

'I used to say: "I'm not tekkin' wor kid, he's ower soft." But I still had to.'

Bobby was the more naturally gifted footballer with grace, style and balance which made him an easy target for the hungry Football League scouts. Jack was a gangling, 6ft 2in tall youth with an ungainly gait and the build of a beanpole.

Jack takes up the story: 'Bobby played for England Boys and every club in the county wanted him while the farthest I got was East Northumberland Boys. I never even played for the county. Not many bet I would make a player. I shook a few people in Ashington when, after serving down the pits, I went off to Leeds and played in their first team at 17. But I'd got that much stronger.'

According to Cissie only Leeds wanted Jack. The world fancied Bobby but it was Manchester United who got him after their scout Joe Armstrong saw him play for Northumberland Boys in 1953.

Both were to enjoy unparalleled success at club and international level, Jack in a bristling Leeds United side under Don Revie and Bobby in a free-flowing Manchester United team bossed by Sir Matt Busby.

Cissie, snowy-haired and in her late seventies, admits: 'Of my four sons Jack's nature is the closest to my own. He is very straight talking and doesn't soft pedal if he thinks I'm wrong, while the others would perhaps try to spare my feelings. By the same token I have to have my say too.

'In his early days at Leeds Jack was stubborn, argumentative and rebellious. He found it hard to settle and find his best form. He clashed with coaches and managers time and time again. Eventually it was two years of national service in the Guards which taught him the real meaning and value of discipline.'

Cissie used to send Jack ten bob notes in her letters while he was in the army. 'They were lovely to have but I didn't really need them,' he says.

When Jack first arrived at Elland Road he played full-back but when the legendary John Charles was on leave from the army he went to centre-half to play directly against him in a practice match. He was only 17 but must have impressed because he remained at No. 5 for the rest of his career.

'We had two or three years together — me at centre-half and John at centre-forward — before John went off to Italy and we won promotion to the First Division in season 1955-56.

'Big John had the biggest single influence on a game of any player I've ever known. You could play ten donkies with him and he'd still run the match for you.'

Bobby's career was a colourful tapestry made up of hundreds of games and dozens of goals. Many were memorable, some unforgettable even from the earliest days when he was just a carefree kid whose greatest joy was hitting the ball hard.

At an obscure F.A. Youth Cup match in March of 1956, for instance, between Manchester United and Bexleyheath a ball came across to the 18-year-old Charlton, who was standing with his back to the goal inside the penalty area. As the ball reached him about chest high he jumped, executed a horizontal roll and scissor-kicked to hit the ball in with his right foot, finishing upright again as it hit the net.

By October of the same year he was in United's senior side for the first time and once again goals — two of them — marked the occasion in a 4-2 win over, appropriately, Charlton Athletic.

Two years on and tragedy was to hit Bobby Charlton and Manchester United. On February 6, 1958 on a snow-covered runway in Munich the plane carrying United's magnificent young team from European Cup glory in Belgrade crashed, killing several passengers. The Busby Babes were destroyed, some lost forever. It was the biggest single tragedy to hit a British soccer team and the news stunned a nation.

Tommy Taylor dead. Roger Byrne dead. Eddie Coleman dead. David Pegg, Mark Jones, Billy Whelan and Geoff Bent dead. Coach Bert Whalley, trainer Tom Curry and secretary Walter Crickmer dead. Big Duncan Edwards and Matt Busby fighting for their lives.

Twice the plane had attempted to take off and the third time ploughed through the perimeter fence at the end of the runway and demolished a house. Miraculously some passengers were thrown clear as the aircraft was torn apart. Among them was Bobby. He had been sitting next to Dennis Viollet near the front of the chartered BEA Elizabethan. In the impact he was thrown clear and landed 100 yards from the wrecked plane still strapped in his seat. His only physical injury was a gashed head but terrible emotional turmoil was still to come as the scale of the tragedy became clear.

When I spoke at length to Jack more than three decades later about the crash his face still clouded over.

'I was particularly close to our kid at that time because we were young players making our way in the game and the news of the crash shattered me. I found out about it in the cruellest of ways. We'd just finished training at Leeds and I was standing in the dressing-room with not a stitch on. All the lads were getting dressed when suddenly the door opened and secretary Arthur Crowther stuck his head round. "The Manchester United plane's crashed," he said. "They don't know if there are any survivors."

'He never looked at me once, just slammed the door shut behind him. I was rooted to the spot. I couldn't say a thing. The silence was only broken when one of the lads said: "Hey, Jack. Your brother's on it, isn't he?"

'Somehow I stumbled into my clothes and ran along to the secretary's office. Only then did they realise the full implications.

'They phoned a few newspapers to find out exactly what had happened but all they knew was that there had been some survivors. They didn't know who they were. I don't know why but I felt I must get home to Ashington. I collected my wife, Pat, and we grabbed a train to Newcastle. All the blokes on the train were talking about was the air disaster. It was awful. I just kept quiet and prayed.

'When we arrived at the Central Station we caught a taxi to the Haymarket to get the bus to Ashington. We were crossing the road when I saw a newseller with a bundle of *Evening Chronicles* under his arm shouting "Munich air crash. Read all about it — all the news."

'I was desperate to find out about our kid yet fearful to buy a paper. In the end I pulled a few coins out of my pocket, grabbed a paper, and scanned page one. There it was: "Robert Charlton, survivor," That was enough. I got the bus home to Cissie and Bob.'

Cissie had found out about the crash through a friend Ted Cockburn, who ran the local newagent's shop. He'd received bills from the *Evening Chronicle* about Bobby being involved and he ran whitefaced to tell Cissie before putting them up outside the shop. Fear gripped at her stomach, the fear of a mother who could have lost a beloved son, before a little while later local bobby Bob Turbill arrived waving a piece of paper. It was a note from Bobby relayed through the Foreign Office. It read: 'Alive and well, see you later' and was signed 'Bobby'.

In the turmoil that followed Duncan Edwards, a wonderful talent, was to lose his life though somehow Matt Busby pulled through. The emotion was to tear at Bobby's guts.

'I knew all the Manchester United lads through Bobby,' said Jack. 'I'd got married just a month before and players like Eddie Coleman, Billy Whelan and Tommy Taylor had been at the wedding. David Pegg used to stay at Ashington with our kid. He was buried just outside Doncaster and I was at the funeral.'

Out of the depths of despair slowly and surely rose a new Manchester United. The music was sweet and Bobby led the orchestra with El Beatle, George Best, who tormented and mesmerised girl fans as much as opposing defenders. There was also the rapier thrust of Denis Law, arm raised in triumph as the ball hit the back of the net; the toothless little grin of Nobby Stiles; and the silky passing skills of Pat Crerand. They won the F.A. Cup, First Division championship and the European Cup, feats which money has been unable to buy since.

When Bobby and Bestie were at their height Old Trafford was the only ground I could go to with Newcastle United, sit back, and enjoy a thrashing for the Geordies. The breathtaking skills compensated so much for the hurt.

The European Cup was won joyously against Benfica and Eusebio at Wembley in 1968 with Bobby Charlton typically scoring one of the four goals, not with a thunderous shot on the run this time but, believe it or not, a deft header! It was ten years after Munich and Bobby believed: 'We were destined to lift Europe's biggest trophy.'

Jack, like Bobby, knew the sweet taste of success with his club. Leeds United were never loved as much as Manchester United, because within their ranks was a steeliness and an attitude which offended the purists but, my, how they could play. Jack is fiercely protective of the much-maligned Don Revie and what he achieved at Elland Road.

'He was a bloody good manager. Look at his record with Leeds. It can't lie. He did the business. We were called the most professional side in the world as though that was a set of dirty words. But we were proud of it. I'm certain that Leeds side will be remembered as one of the greatest ever and I'm thrilled about that.'

Perhaps the secret of Bobby and Jack Charlton as players — apart from natural ability — is that they both played for managers they rated totally. Bobby, insists his mam, would have run through a brick wall for Matt Busby, whose policy was: 'You can all play — so go out and do it.'

Bobby did it 604 times in the Football League for Manchester United, scoring a record 199 goals. For England he won 106 caps and notched 49 goals, another record.

Those are the facts. Matt Busby adds the opinion of soccer's legions when he says: 'The name of Bobby Charlton will stand for ever. Time will undoubtedly add to his stature rather than diminish it.

'He has broken all records and won everything possible there is to win. Yet he has remained completely unspoiled, still prepared to do more than his fair share for the cause of Manchester United.'

Bobby will also be remembered as a scrupulously fair player, a man of discipline who rarely if ever troubled the referee's notebook. Terry Hennessy, a driving wing-half with Nottingham Forest, neatly summed up Charlton thus: 'He's a man I fear and respect. Fear because he is such a superb player and respect because he's so clean. When you beat Bobby Charlton fair and square you always know that he won't bring you down from behind. I think it upsets him to see players getting stuck into each other. I remember one day when I was having quite a battle with Denis Law. After one heated exchange Bobby ran up to us and said: "Come on, you two. Don't get involved." And because you respect him you listen to him.'

Muscle was often the only way defenders could think of halting Bobby, of course. Brother Jack chuckles: 'He never liked playing at Bolton. They had a couple of hammer throwers called Roy Hartle and John Higgins who used to give our kid a right seeing to. One day when Leeds hadn't a game I went over to see Manchester United play Bolton. Our kid had fixed the ticket but I was a bit late and so was quite surprised to see Bobby standing at the players' entrance with a huge grin on his face waving frantically at me.

'He had my ticket clutched in his hand and was shouting: "I'm injured. I can't play." He was dead chuffed that Hartle and Higgins weren't going to spend 90 minutes kicking lumps out of him.'

It was with England, however, that the brothers scaled the very peak of soccer's Everest. In 1966, to be precise, when England came through an extra-time thriller with West Germany to lift the World Cup 4-2. A nation rejoiced as it had never done since the end of the Second World War. Wembley was awash with emotion. On the final whistle Bobby and Jack knelt on the pitch hugging each other, Bobby with tears streaming down his face.

'Silly beggar,' said Jack, a teak-hard defender whom you

could never imagine doing such a thing. 'I never cry with emotion. I only cry when I'm angry.'

The match see-sawed through 120 minutes of nerve-wracking tension. England one down, 2-1 up, 2-2 at the death of the 90 minutes and eventually 4-2 after a dispute about whether or not the ball crossed the line for the third goal.

'Germans are always coming up to me and saying we pinched the World Cup — that the ball wasn't over the line,' says Jack. 'But I tell them that their goal which made it 2-2 just before the 90 minutes were up shouldn't have counted because it was handball. It was, too. So whatever way you look at it, we won fairly and squarely.'

His recollection of England's finest feat and its highpoints is still crystal clear: 'When we went ahead in the game for the first time I was up with our attack for some reason. Geoff Hurst, who had scored our opening goal, was out on the flank. Suddenly he checked and crossed the ball. It ricocheted off a defender and, spinning crazily, began dropping towards me at the far post. "Hell," I said to myself, "It's mine — what if I bloody miss?" The goal was wide open but it was a difficult ball to control because of the spin. Keeping your shot down was going to be the problem.

'While I was still in a turmoil Martin Peters came out of nowhere to sweep me to one side and strike the ball unerringly into the net. Was I relieved! But to this day I wonder if I would have scored in the World Cup final or knocked the hat off the bloke at the back of the goal.

'West Germany's equaliser came when I jumped to head the ball. I was whistled up for using an opponent as a platform but I didn't do that. He made a back for me. The free-kick was ten yards outside the penalty area. When the ball was eventually crossed into the box it struck one of the Germans under the arm. That took the pace off the ball and, instead of flying across goal, it dropped down and one of their players beat Ray Wilson to it to knock it in.

'I had a good view from the far post looking across the penalty box and there was no question that the West German knocked it down with his arm. Bobby Moore turned instinctively and shouted "Handball" but the referee gave a goal. If you ever see a film of that final, you'll see I'm right. It was definitely handball.'

Hurst was to go on to become the first ever player to score a hat-trick in a World Cup final, thanks to Moore, the skipper at the shoulder of Jack Charlton.

'With literally only seconds to go Moore pulled the ball down on the edge of our six-yard box. I was screaming at him to clear the ball. The veins were standing out on my neck. But Bobby took not a blind bit of notice. He looked up, played the ball calmly to Alan Ball, then called for it back. He got it and moved forward before releasing an inch-perfect pass to Hurst who ran on to complete his hat-trick. It was unbelievable. Me — I would have belted the ball as hard as I could towards the opponents' corner flag. But Moore had style and class.'

I know the Charltons well. Cissie, I must admit, is a favourite . . . a lovely, warm, cuddly lady with twinkling eyes who, when I nervously tried to pay a personal tribute to Jackie Milburn at a memorial service for him in Ashington, hugged me when I returned to the pew next to her and said: 'Aye, pet. Jackie would have loved that.'

Bobby and Jack, no longer quite as close as they were in their early playing days, are different people. I've worked with both of them doing chat shows in the North East . . . Bobby is slightly distant and more serious, a man who now lives in the stockbroker belt of Cheshire and mixes accordingly. Jack is bright and down to earth, doesn't stand fools gladly, but is quite prepared to put on his cloth cap and go down to the local social club for a pint.

Yet he socialises with royalty and landed gentry when on one of his regular shoots. Put wellies on him and a gun under his arm and he's as happy as Larry. He's big mates with the Earl of Harewood, regularly shooting on the estate.

His attitude to football and his pursuit of the outdoor life was made more than clear when I took him to lunch just after his appointment as Newcastle United's manager.

'Remember it's only a game,' Big Jack told me, tucking into his steak. 'I've no intention of dying in the dug-out like dear old Jock Stein [he collapsed and died at the end of a Scotland match]. There'll be days when I'll simply not be around.'

A week into the season, with United top of the First Division after three successive wins, he took himself off to fish on the River Tay near Dundee and commuted to matches at Arsenal and Manchester United! That's why the job as manager of the Republic of Ireland is so perfect for him . . . he can utilise his considerable coaching ability to the full, hasn't to bother with the hassle of the transfer market, and can indulge in his love of the countryside whenever he wants.

At the end of the same lunch I drove Jack back to United's training ground at Benwell. He was still clenching a half-finished cigar in his teeth as we strode over to where the players were holding a practice match. As we stood watching for a moment a ball was played into the penalty area and was only half cleared by a defender with his head.

'No, no, no,' bellowed Charlton striding onto the pitch and stopping the game. 'Here, knock a ball into me.' He stood in the penalty area, mud squelching over his suede shoes and cigar still firmly in place. Over came the ball and he rose like a bird to head it powerfully almost to the halfway line without choking on the cigar. 'That's the bloody way to do it,' he said striding back over to join me.

A further insight into Jack Charlton the man came at a talk-in we held at Washington. The club was packed to the rafters with Newcastle and Sunderland fans and Roker boss Len Ashurst, sharing the stage with us, was diplomacy himself. But when the first question came to Big Jack he stood up and announced: 'Let's get one thing straight. I don't care what you think, so I want no arguments when I answer any questions.'

Ashurst cringed and the audience got on its hind legs (you know the sort of thing, 'I know you don't care about what we think but . . .'). It was a lively evening to say the least, yet Big Jack walked off stage at the end, went up to the bar for a pint, and declared: 'That was champion! I enjoyed it.'

The same man can be warm, with a beaming smile that lights up his full face. When the miners' strike was in full swing from March, 1984 to March, 1985 Jack regularly gave away free tickets for the Newcastle matches to miners. No doubt his own background in the pit town of Ashington made him a ready sympathiser and led to him becoming a firm friend of their union leader Arthur Scargill, who had lived near Jack during his time as manager of Sheffield Wednesday.

Jack may be a World Cup winner with England but they love him even more deeply in the south of Ireland where he's lifted their international football team to heights never before achieved. Previously the Republic had been a team of non-achievers producing the occasional master craftsman such as Johnny Giles and Liam Brady capable of delighting the eye. But under the big Geordie a team pattern was moulded which sacrificed individual flair for overall effect and Dublin, used to seeing the north produce all the eye-catching results, suddenly had something to shout about themselves.

Charlton produced his first piece of success when the Republic reached the finals of the European Championships in 1988 and then went on to a memorable victory over England. But more, much more, was to be achieved. Ireland not only reached the World Cup finals for the first time in their history in 1990 but went on to battle their way through to the last eight. They stayed longer in soccer's greatest tournament than the likes of Brazil, Holland, Russia, Uruguay, Spain and Scotland, eventually losing by the closest of margins, 1-0, to hosts Italy in Rome's Olympic Stadium.

In the final week Big Jack and his jolly green giants beat Romania in a heart-stopping penalty shoot-out, met the Pope at the Vatican, and returned home to upstage freedom fighter Nelson Mandela with the size of their welcome at Dublin Airport.

A huge crowd estimated at 250,000 turned out to greet their unlikely hero, an Englishman who still lived on Tyneside. He was told he could be President if he so wished. He didn't. He just wanted to go fishing!

# Cardinal Basil Hume

## Archbishop of Westminster

FIVE little Humes were brought up in the Jesmond home which also doubled as father's surgery — Madelaine, Christine, George, Frances and John. Their mother, Lady Hume, was a Roman Catholic, while father Sir William, an eminent heart specialist and professor of medicine, was Church of England. Little George, whom his father hoped might grow up to be a footballer, actually became Cardinal Basil Hume, Archbishop of Westminster and leader of five million Roman Catholics in England and Wales.

George (his monastic name is Basil) was, perhaps appropriately, an angelic little boy. At four months he was picked up by his French great-grandmother demanding to know: 'Will somebody tell me what is the matter with this child? He's the only one I know that never cries!'

His eldest sister Madelaine, wife of Lord Hunt, formerly Sir John Hunt, Cabinet secretary and three years George's senior, recalls: 'Yes, he was a very good little boy. Indeed I'm told that at the age of three he would say things like: "Oh, I DO love making people happy. I DO love seeing them smile!" '

The Humes were brought up in a fairly strict routine at an elegant four-storey home in Ellison Place, Newcastle very near a sardine-canning factory, but they were aware of children running barefoot around the city. They remember the terrible, hungry twenties and thirties and were made to realise how privileged their own family life was.

Running up and down and sliding on floors wasn't tolerated in the old days at Ellison Place. The children were told endlessly not to make a noise and upset the patients — one of the disadvantages of living over a surgery. Every Christmas Day was spent in the wards of Newcastle's Royal Victoria Infirmary helping the nurses hand out the food. Father would carve the turkey in the men's wards and then cope with the plum pudding in the women's wards. Perhaps it was George's early life, being brought up on depressed Tyneside the son of a doctor, that gave him the understanding of people he shows today.

There was a great deal of fun, too, playing with hoops in St. Thomas's Park, and the occasional treat of being allowed to walk down to Fenwick's or the Grainger Market, the endless walks with a governess or nanny and the jolly French-style Sundays when, after Mass, they would play cards or football and enjoy themselves as weekdays never allowed.

There was never any religious conflict in the well-ordered Hume household. Lady Marie Hume, who was born in Paris, took her five children and their nanny off to Mass while their father was doing his rounds at the RVI.

Lady Hume may have prayed for her elder son to be a priest but Sir William, his father, probably prayed just as hard for him to become a footballer. Never was he more proud than when one of the teachers at George's prep school told him that the boy had all the makings of a first-class footballer. That love of our national sport was to stay with Basil Hume even after he was enthroned as the Archbishop of Westminster in 1976. He's a lifelong Newcastle United supporter who has been known to regularly rush home to watch *Match of the Day*. After football comes music (he writes his sermons to classical music), squash and fishing.

At the age of 10 George was befriended by a Dominican priest and visited the poorer parts of Tyneside. He wanted to be a Dominican and work among such people but at Ampleforth College, one of England's oldest public schools, he switched his attention from the Dominicans to the Benedictines who also worked among the poor in the many northern industrial parishes they ran. By the time he was old enough to join the order, though, he had another choice to make. It was 1941 and he could have gone to war. He had, he later admitted, a rather romantic view of his calling and imagined himself sharing the sufferings of people in a bombed-out or even occupied Britain. He chose the Abbey and was therefore exempt from service, something he rather regretted later. Instead of the army — or more probably the navy — he began to study for the priesthood. Ampleforth maintained a house, St. Benet's Hall in Oxford, and it was there that he studied history for his first degree.

From Oxford Father Basil went to Fribourg in Switzerland to study for a licentiate in theology, his superiors no doubt calculating that his fluency in French would be of some significant help. French was more than a second language to him — he would not address his mother in anything else right up until her death in 1978.

Ordained and qualified, the young Father Basil was not then sent to work in the slums of Liverpool as he had once hoped but put to work to teach modern languages to the boys and dogmatic theology to junior monks, and to coach the school rugby team. He recalls 40 boys crowding into his room as housemaster to watch *Top of the Pops* on television while he studied Aquinas in one corner, trying to grasp one of the proofs of the existence of God.

From housemaster to abbot in 1963 was his first and only step up the ecclesiastical ladder until a phone call from the apostlic delegate in February of 1976 informed him that he was to succeed the late Cardinal Heenan as Archbishop of Westminster. The shock of his appointment sent a ripple round the Catholic church. He was an outsider, promoted over the heads of a solid hierarchy. The first monk to preside at Westminster in 125 years.

The news surprised even him. It came as he was eating dinner. He didn't enjoy the rest of the meal. 'It astonished me because I hadn't cut a public figure,' he admitted afterwards. 'I hadn't even written anything.'

His family were equally surprised. When the announcement was made by Pope Paul his eldest sister Lady Hunt said: 'We were all shocked, not because we thought he couldn't do the job but because we had never dreamed such a thing would happen. It was easy for mother to visualise him as Abbot of Ampleforth because she knew Ampleforth. But she had never lived in London and she hadn't been near an Archbishop in the whole of her life so it was rather difficult for her.'

To the outside world celibacy is one of the greatest burdens a monk must carry. For Cardinal Basil Hume, 53 when he was enthroned in Westminster Cathedral, it was also a problem. A man with an affectionate nature, who gets on well with most of the people he meets, he admits that he's attracted to women.

'Celibacy is a sacrifice,' he says. 'You cannot be a true celibate unless you are mature and well balanced. A successful celibate is warm and affectionate in his relationships with other people but disciplined. Like everyone else he has to have a very positive and sane view of sex, to see it in the context of true love.

'The problems change with age. When one is younger the sex impulse is stronger. When one is older one experiences the absence of a close one-to-one relationship. This absence can drive the celibate to a very considerable loneliness and unhappiness. This is where prayer comes in.'

His advice to priests was to behave towards women friends as a mature man who was head over heels in love with his own wife would treat them, never wanting to do anything to hurt or betray himself. That draws the line at physical sex but gives considerable freedom to the emotions.

Father Basil accepted his new job 'under obedience' as a monk. 'A monk doesn't choose what he does. He does what he is told by the authorites above him. And what I felt about it was, as far as I was concerned as a monk, irrelevant.'

His ability with throw-away lines, his readiness to be self-mocking, were amply illustrated during his many Press conferences at the time of his appointment. Asked if he had ever met the Pope he replied: 'No — but then I'm very small fry!'

A man of vision, he counted among his friends the Archbishop of Canterbury, Dr Coggan, had preached in several Methodist chapels, and had a lot of contact with the Society of Friends who were strong in Yorkshire. He attempted to break down barriers, receiving a standing ovation when he became the first Roman Catholic Archbishop of Westminster to address the General Synod of the Church of England in 1978 . . . . 'divided Christianity is a scandal. Our divisions are a stumbling block and diminish the credibility of Christ's message to the world.'

Similarly a year later Cardinal Hume became the first Roman Catholic to preach at Durham Cathedral for 400 years.

Inevitably, his home town was to recognise one of their great sons and in 1980, at a special ceremony to mark Newcastle's 900th anniversary, he was made an honorary Freeman of the City . . . and fulfilled a 30-year ambition. Similarly honoured that day was Jackie Milburn, a legendary footballer with Newcastle United and England. Wor Jackie, as he was affectionately known, had helped bring the F.A. Cup back to Tyneside three times in five years during the early 1950s and the soccer-loving Archbishop admitted: 'I've waited 30 years for his autograph!'

Wor Jackie, as Geordie as they come, had been Cardinal Hume's hero — 'he was a star and a real gentleman' — and a strong friendship was to flourish. The Archbishop recorded a special interview when Wor Jackie was the subject of *This is Your Life* a year later, and when he was lying terminally ill with cancer in 1988 the private, loving letters Cardinal Hume sent to Jackie's Ashington home greatly helped to lift the suffering and the depression. Jackie's widow, Laura, has proudly kept them to this very day. I've been privileged to see them and the warmth and humility of the writer is something which reaches out beyond any religious barriers.

# Ian La Frenais

A CHANCE meeting at a party in the Uxbridge Arms, Notting Hill Gate in 1962 turned two careers into one and produced literally hundreds of half-hour situation comedies, countless films and West End theatre successes.

Mike Burridge, who later became a lecturer at the London School of Economics, introduced Ian La Frenais to Dick Clement. At the time La Frenais was down from Newcastle and staying in the flat above Burridge in Holland Park. Clement was a trainee at the BBC.

It was, says Clement, a very boring evening. Says La Frenais: 'I thought Dick was very strange and intellectual. And he used to eat out a lot!'

From that chance encounter developed one of the most prodigious writing partnerships in British comedy. Two basically different personalities merged to fit together like a glove. Clement the married one with the house, the children and the dogs; La Frenais the young man about town mad keen on football and music and a regular visitor to London's celebrated nightspots such as Tramp.

Success came almost instantly. At the end of his traineeship Clement had to produce a programme almost like a student takes an exam to show what he's learned and turned up with 'The Likely Lads'!

'In those days most trainees used to do 20 minutes of video with a group or a musician,' recalls La Frenais, 'but Dick suggested that we write a piece of situation comedy. We already had a sketch about a couple of northern lads who were discussing their dates and which had been performed as an amateur show, so we expanded that. Dick produced it and luckily for us when Dennis Main Wilson went to view it Marty Feldman, who was then a successful writer at the BBC, tagged along with him.

'Marty said: 'Those boys can write. Keep them down,' and the BBC asked us if we thought there was a series in it. Of course we said "Yes" and then, because the producer who was going to do it died Dick produced and directed it as well.'

That was in 1964. Apparently the BBC's attitude at first was 'Well, at least it's cheap', which was the very least that it was. 'When you get such superb luck it's like getting a great hand at poker,' said Clement. 'You've got to play it well. We knew that it was luck at the time and we were terrified of failing, because we knew that we would never get such a chance again.'

The TV series starred James Bolam and Rodney Bewes, two actors I got to know very well and who produced that essential spark between them on screen without ever being particularly good friends off it. Bolam, from Sunderland, was the introvert who shunned personal stardom, preferring to suffer for his art while Yorkshireman Bewes, perhaps the less naturally gifted, enjoyed his fame to the full.

'The Likely Lads' won La Frenais and Clement the Screenwriters' Guild award for the best television series of the year. While it was based essentially on Ian's Tyneside upbringing, it wasn't until the follow-up series 'Whatever Happened To The Likely Lads' that the Geordie connection was given full rein with location shots featuring areas like Blaydon, Whickham and Killingworth.

The likely lad with the unlikely Geordie name of La Frenais was born in Monkseaton on the coast at the mouth of the Tyne and educated in Dame Allan's School in the city of Newcastle. Following National Service in Aldershot — 'undistinguished,' he says — he worked as a cigarette salesman until the sheer futility of it all persuaded him to pack his bags and head for London to seek the proverbial fame and fortune.

Ian used to turn out for Rockcliff rugby club, and although he did the usual young man's round of pubs, dances and jazz clubs, most of his social life was spent in the atmosphere of the rugger club.

He was 22 when he took the A1 south. It was the height of the swinging 60's and television's newest and brightest scriptwriter fell easily into the lifestyle. Flared trousers, open-necked shirt (he hated wearing ties) and long black locks epitomised the young man of the era. A bachelor pad in Chelsea and a Rolls Royce were the trappings of success . . . once on a visit home to Newcastle we were stopped by an alert traffic warden as we approached Ian's roller because he couldn't believe that two lads in jeans could own such a car!

Tragically Ian's dad Cyril only lived long enough to see his son's initial success. He died of a heart attack in 1967 as 'The Likely Lads' hit our screens.

But his mam Gladys, who lived in a luxury flat in Beacon House just round the corner from me in Whitley Bay, was able to enjoy Ian's triumphs to the full. A lovely lady known as 'Auntie Glad' to all of us, she would entertain his showbiz friends whenever they came north with him. Many's the super night I've had sitting around with the likes of Rodney Bewes, Tom Courtenay and Ian with Auntie Glad fussing over us like a mother hen pouring out the glasses of red wine. A one off, when she died in 1977 she requested that men only attend her funeral in Whitley Bay and Ian, her only son, made certain her wish was granted.

The La Frenais-Clement team went on from 'The Likely Lads' to produce 'The Further Adventures of Lucky Jim' for the Beeb and then branched into films, chalking up successes with 'The Jokers', starring Michael Crawford and Oliver Reed; 'Otley' starring Tom Courtenay which won them the Screenwriters' Guild award for film of the year; 'Hannibal Brooks', another Oliver Reed film; 'Villain' with Richard Burton; and 'Catch Me a Spy', starring Kirk Douglas. La Frenais also worked, without Dick Clement, on 'The Virgin Soldiers.'

Soccer was his big love away from his writing. That and pop music, which saw him write the theme songs for a lot of his shows and gather around him such rock and rollers as Mick Jagger, Ronnie Wood, Bill Wyman, Rod Stewart and Keith Moon. He even went on Elton John's historic trip to Russia to make a film of the tour.

Not surprisingly his great love was — and still is — Newcastle United, though living in London his adopted team was Chelsea. Indeed his pad overlooked Stamford Bridge. At the time

I was travelling with United for the *Evening Chronicle* and Ian would entertain us whenever we were in the capital, arranging private film shows etc.

I well remember one special weekend in 1974 when United played Liverpool in the F.A. Cup final at Wembley. On the Wednesday his musical 'Billy', starring Michael Crawford, opened in Drury Lane. The following night he and United skipper Bob Moncur were my guests at the Football Writers' Association annual dinner and on the Friday he entertained a Newcastle United party of 35 at his show.

On the Saturday he was at Wembley, just as he had been at St. James's Park for the third round and at Hillsborough for an epic semi-final. He sat in the stands with the players' wives and afterwards attended the club's official banquet along with myself. And to round off a momentous five days on the Sunday the very first episode of another smash hit series, 'Porridge', was recorded in London.

'Porridge' was an absolute winner, a vintage piece of television comedy so popular that repeats were still being shown 16 years later. Along with Dick, Ian created Norman Stanley Fletcher, Officer Mackay and the closed community of H.M. Prison Slade. The success of the series was due largely to the brilliance of Ronnie Barker, who played the experienced old lag Fletcher, though there were other key performances from the late Richard Beckinsale, the late Fulton Mackay, Brian Wilde as Officer Barraclough and Peter Vaughan as the prison godfather Grout. It was an unusual vehicle for a comedy — life behind bars in a grim prison — but it worked a treat.

The series was shot mainly in and around Chelmsford Prison, empty at the time because a fire had caused inmates to be transferred to other prisons.

'The Home Office, the Governor and the prison officers were very co-operative,' said Ian. 'It's debatable whether the film could have been made at all if we'd not been allowed inside Chelmsford.'

Ian had a habit of including the names of his mates back home in his scripts. John Gibson played in skiffle band, United full-back Frank Clark cropped up as a potential best man for

Rodney Bewes in 'The Likely Lads', and Bob Moncur and Malcolm Macdonald also got mentions.

Often I would receive calls at the *Evening Chronicle* from all over the world asking if I could check out some minor details in the office library. A typical example was when Ian was writing a musical on Laurel and Hardy — Stan Laurel had spent some of his early years in South Shields and Ian, ever a stickler for reality, needed to know some background.

The special talent of La Frenais and Clement was always going to take them away from the confines of London and by 1976 they were domiciled in Los Angeles.

'It wasn't for tax reasons,' explained Ian. 'Simply because progression in our work meant living in Los Angeless to be at the hub of things. The film industry in England was so small. You've got to be where the head office is.'

La Frenais bought actress Gayle Hunnicutt's old house on Hutton Drive in Beverly Hills where he lived with his French girlfriend Doris, whose brother-in-law is rock singer Johnny Halliday. They eventually got wed quietly.

Looking back years later Ian told me: 'Moving to Hollywood was an unbelievable risk. I mean our reputation counted for nothing out there. We didn't mean a thing. People perceived the move as a sign of luxury and success but it wasn't. It was an act of courage. We put our ass on the line. We could have lost all the money we had acquired. But then we do things that surprise people. Like going off to Russia with Elton John and filming his tour. We'd be much richer if we channelled our efforts differently but that isn't the way we see things.'

La Frenais is a man who sprints through life while others walk. He is an outgoing type with a waspish sense of humour. He is also a bit of a gypsy who tends to sleep wherever his head rests. Often the back of his Rolls Royce was full of clothes and his shaving gear and he would doss at a friend's house.

One of his most famous quotes when asked if he missed the North East was: 'When I'm sitting by the pool in Beverly Hills and it's 80 degrees and there are a lot of beautiful girls in bikinis around, North Shields somehow doesn't seem too attractive!'

That was typical La Frenais humour. In fact he never lost his love for Britain or for Geordieland. When in London he often stayed with Tony Charles, who used to be in the rag trade but later joined Ian's firm, the aptly named Witzend Productions, and became a producer of such telly shows as 'Shine on Harvey Moon'. Tony's wife Audrey was born in North Shields, and so trips home to Tyneside were frequent for all three of them.

If La Frenais and Clement have succeeded beyond their wildest dreams, then unquestionably one of the main reasons is that they have never forgotten their roots. They have the common touch, the ability to write convincingly about ordinary people. That was never better underlined than when from the opulence of America they produced 'Auf Wiedersehen Pet' in 1984.

The hit TV series was conceived by a North Easterner and sold as an idea to a Geordie. From then on it was nourished and developed and finally written in Los Angeles with visits to Düsseldorf in search of reality.

Film director Franc Roddam, who hails from Stockton, regailed similarly expatriate writers La Frenais and Clement with tales of a Geordie bricklayer who had worked on a building site in Düsseldorf. The idea fascinated La Frenais and out of it came the story of a bunch of Brits existing in Stalag quarters, deprived of home and family and faced with the unenviable prospect of coping with the Krauts and Turks. The wimpish Neville, dependable Dennis and loutish, foul-mouthed Oz were born.

' "Auf Wiedersehen Pet" was two years in the making,' Ian told me when I went down to London for a party to mark the launch. 'We had to write 13 hours of television which is a mammoth exercise. It's much more helpful to work with a long-term writer on the characters to help create them and bring them to life. I think of myself as Dr. Frankenstein and Oz is my monster.

'It seemed logical for our three main characters to go out to Germany from a deeply depressed area so the North East fitted our requirements.'

Writing a huge TV series isn't simply a matter of coming up with several plots interwoven into every script. A writer must also think of the financial side of the operation.

'It's essential to write to a budget,' La Frenais told me. 'For financial reasons we had to have a lot more scenes set in the hut than out in the streets of Düsseldorf. I knew by the time I was writing the later episodes that we couldn't go back to Germany again for location work, for example, so I had to place the characters somewhere safe.

'Dick and I wrote three episodes together and then Dick went off directing and I wrote the next seven on my own. I was very nervous about it — this was an hour-long show, not a sitcom, and if it didn't work it would have meant hour upon hour of watching your work go down the pan.

'With "Porridge" we knew that Ronnie Barker had a legacy and we were fairly confident but here we were in the main dealing with unknown actors.'

The casting, however, turned out to be a masterstroke. The magnificent seven of Jimmy Nail, Tim Healy, Kevin Whatley, Gary Holton, Timothy Spall, Christopher Fairbank and Pat Roach came together like a jigsaw puzzle.

'Dick and I saw the short list,' said Ian. 'I knew Tim Healy's work from the World Cup film he did with Dennis Waterman and I'd met Gary Holton through his wife's ex-husband. But Jimmy Nail was new off the streets. He was magic.'

However, as with all TV writers, La Frenais had to develop some characters as they became stronger in front of the cameras and cut back on the dialogue of others who obviously couldn't hold centre stage. Out of it all rose Oz, who had so many of the best lines and most irretrievable situations. Remember him recounting his experiences in the local Düsseldorf brothel: 'Why man, sex is in its infancy in Gateshead . . . .'

Jimmy Nail, one of three Geordie actors in the series along with Healy and Whatley, was splendid as the awful loutish Oz and it didn't hinder him one little bit that his background was so similar to the series under construction. Jimmy had worked as a labourer for three years in Germany and had been self-employed buying, gutting, refurbishing and then reselling houses in Newcastle.

I remember La Frenais recalling with a twinkle in his eye how he cast Nail in the part. 'We'd been looking everywhere for an Oz when suddenly the door opened, Jimmy stuck his head round, and said: ''Hey, is this the reet place for the auditions, then?'' in as broad a Geordie accent as you could hear. Straight away I said: ''He's Oz!'' '

Jimmy's surname is really Bradford but as a kid he was hard as nails with the looks to match. Hence his stage name. In fact his background was in music — later he had a hit record — and he'd been in a local rock and roll band called the Crabs. One of his gags was: 'I'm going on tour with the crabs!'

Nail's dislike of the Press is legendary but I've always found him a great fella . . . unpretentious with a love of jeans and a T shirt and a ready wit to defuse any situation.

When first introduced he told me: 'I know you all right — I saw you at Heaton Buffs doing a talk-in with Bob Moncur. Asked you how the lads would go, didn't I?'

Nail loves his football. His old man, he told me, played for Huddersfield Town and as a schoolboy he himself was offered a trial with Newcastle United.

'I didn't turn up and they never let me play for the school again,' he said with a grimace. He supported United from the terraces for many years and talks about the team like a terrace punter.

Being expelled from school prevented him becoming an English teacher, he insists, and he also considered being a copper at one time. Oz as a boy in blue. . . what a thought!

La Frenais mocked him gently, saying: 'Well, you're a bit of a megalomaniac, aren't you?'

Tim Healy — Dennis, the leader of the pack in 'Auf Wiedersehen Pet' — was born not a hut's length away from me in Benwell. Like La Frenais, he clings proudly to his Geordie background and actually still lives up here at Stocksfield. But then Jimmy Nail has also bought a house in South Gosforth to use as his second base.

'Ian's ability to give an actor so much meat to work on is marvellous,' says Healy. 'The success of the series was phenomenal. I'm recognised everywhere I go now (though everyone calls me Dennis) after years of being able to shop unnoticed in Woolies and the British Home Stores!'

A second series of 'Pet' took the lads to Spain but

production was hit when Gary Holton, who played a lustful Cockney, tragically died of a drugs overdose during shooting. La Frenais and Clement decided to keep in the Holton scenes already in the can and rewrite the parts still to be shot to exclude him from the action. It was a tricky situation but such was the skill of the pen that the finished article looked totally pre-planned.

Tim and Jimmy have become good friends through Ian and their love of sport has given us a lot of common ground.

While Healy embarked on a major TV series in Australia early in 1990, La Frenais and Nail were getting together to work on another TV blockbuster. The idea was Jimmy's . . . a Geordie cop in London, disgraced and sent back home to work undercover. 'Spender' was the ideal vehicle for Nail and, with the help of La Frenais, 10 hours of scripts went into production on Tyneside in early April.

Another surefire winner with a heavy emphasis on Geordies was about to hit our screens.

# David Scott Cowper

WHAT is the definition of courage? There are many acts of heroism perpetrated by man but, without question, one of them must be challenging mountainous seas in howling gales alone in a small yacht tossed around like a bit of flotsam.

The aching loneliness, the months at sea with nothing but gulls and fish for company, the lack of sleep, the cramped, uncomfortable conditions, the continual possibility of danger and personal injury or illness. All add to the courage of a lone round-the-world sailor. One such man is Tyneside's epic adventurer David Scott Cowper who has even surpassed such English giants of the sea as Sir Francis Chichester, Robin Knox-Johnston and Chay Blyth. Not that you would know if you talked to the Newcastle-born chartered surveyor who, in common with a lot of great men, simply plays down his achievements. If you listened to Scott Cowper you could be excused for thinking he had just come from a trip round the local boating lake.

In fact this 48-year-old family man is a record breaker, a man who has overcome incredible odds to not only survive but write his name into the record books. A single-minded man who has made his personal dreams come true at a huge financial cost to himself.

Take a big gulp and then wade through his greatest achievements — the first ever person to circumnavigate the world west to east and east to west via Cape Horn; the first person to circumnavigate the world by powered vessel singlehanded; the first ever person to complete three true circumnavigations; the first ever transit of the North West Passage singlehanded; the first ever to enter the Pacific from the Atlantic or vice versa; and the first ever person to circumnavigate the world via the North West Passage.

In the first of his epic trips, round the world west to east in April of 1980, he shattered by 23 days the 272-day record of Dame Naomi James and also clipped two days off the late Sir Francis Chichester's 1967 record of 226 days spent actually at sea.

Two years later Scott Cowper circled the world the wrong way round — the hard way — in his trusty 40-foot Bermudan Sloop *Ocean Bound*, cracking the record by 38 days held by a Japanese sailor and, in the process, destroying by an astonishing 71 days Chay Blyth's east-west record of 292 days' actual sailing time.

The man from the banks of the Tyne had beaten Dame Naomi, Sir Francis Chichester and Chay Blyth. . . yet he couldn't swim and was chronically seasick if he put a leg over the bow. To a landlubber such apparent restrictions are mindboggling and only add to the obvious deep-rooted courage and determination of the man.

Yet David himself doesn't see either fact as particularly mindblowing.

'It's true, I couldn't swim and I suffered from seasickness,' he told me sitting in his office in Newcaslte's city centre, something you felt is a prison to a person who yearns for the wide open expanse of the world's oceans. 'But they were never honestly a draw-back. It's a case of mind over matter.

'For example, you wouldn't survive in rough seas even if you were a good swimmer. You may last a little bit longer but not long enough to make a significant difference.'

Both 'liabilities' are now a thing of the past. His seasickness left him three or four years ago — 'I loved the sea yet suffered seasickness and my sister who hates the sea was never ill' — and he learned to swim late in life only a couple of years ago.

'An Australian who had never had a failure taught me to swim. She gave me more confidence — and the fact that I learned in private rather than in a public swimming pool helped greatly.'

His first truly great adventure had seen him named as one of a dozen Men of the Year at a luncheon in London's swish Savoy Hotel along with the likes of actor Sir Alec Guinness, diplomat Lord Soames and playwright Tom Stoppard, but if you press him on his finest achievement he'll plump for his 1982 feat of circumnavigating the globe from east to west.

Little Katie McMullen pictured with her granny sitting at the front door.

*Below:* Catherine Cookson with Eamonn Andrews on the set of television's *This is Your Life* in 1982.

Sting (centre) with Stewart Copeland and Andy Summers who, as The Police, dominated the pop charts in the early 80's.

Gordon Sumner (fifth from the left in back row) in the St. Cuthbert's Grammar School rugby team.

Sting being welcomed by fans at the Central Station in Newcastle before being whisked away in a white Rolls Royce to play a sell-out concert.

Brothers in opposition — Bobby Charlton (left) in Manchester United's colours takes on Leeds United centre-half Jack Charlton.

England's World Cup winners of 1966 show off the Jules Rimet Trophy at Wembley — left to right Jack Charlton, Gordon Banks, Roger Hunt, Bobby Moore, George Cohen and Bobby Charlton.

Little George Hume who went on to become the leader of five million Roman Catholics in England and Wales.

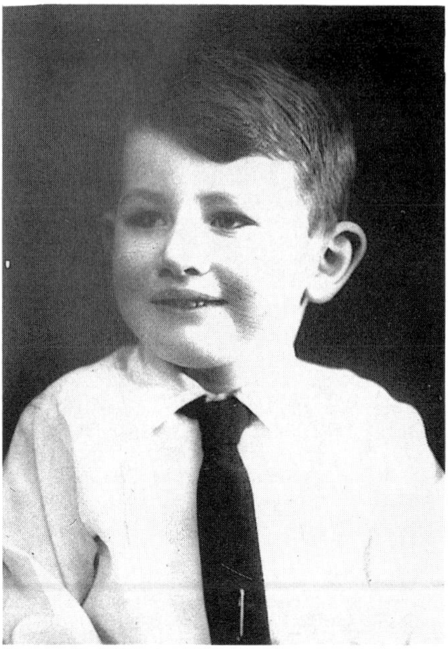

Cardinal Basil Hume with another famous Geordie, footballer Jackie Milburn, on the day they were both made freemen of the city of Newcastle in 1980.

Ian La Frenais (left) and author John Gibson pictured privately in the flat of Ian's mother Gladys in Whitley Bay.

Ian La Frenais, the co-writer of the television hit series 'Auf Wiedersehen Pet', with one of its stars Tim Healy.

David Scott Cowper arrives home on the Tyne in his 40-foot Bermudan Sloop *Ocean Bound* after his first epic voyage round the world west to east in 1980 when he beat the records of Dame Naomi James and Sir Francis Chichester.

Miriam Stoppard on the TV set of her celebrated interview with the Prime Minister Margaret Thatcher.

John Hall, the son of an Ashington miner, shows off the MetroCentre in Gateshead which established his name in property developing.

John and Mae Hall who have built Cameron Hall Development into a company worth between £80m and £100m.

GATESHEAD
804
2049

Brendan Foster receives his BBC Sports Personality of the Year trophy from former world racing driver Jackie Stewart in 1974.

*Left:* Big Bren, wearing his Gateshead vest, leading another top Geordie athlete Mick McLeod (left) in a cross-country race.

*Right:* Author John Gibson presents a young Steve Cram with an Athlete of the Month award in 1978 after Cram had set a world mile record for a 17-year-old in the Emsley Carr Mile. Behind are some of Steve's trophies in his parents' house in Jarrow.

Prince Edward presents Steve Cram with his gold medal after winning the 800 metres at the Commonwealth Games of 1986.

The Princess of Wales shares a joke with Rowan Atkinson after a Royal Variety performance at London's Victoria Palace Theatre.

*on next page:*
Rowan Atkinson in his award-winning role as Blackadder on TV.

The Princess of Wales shares a joke with Rowan Atkinson after a Royal Variety performance at London's Victoria Palace Theatre.

*on next page:*
Rowan Atkinson in his award-winning role as Blackadder on TV.

'That's the difficult way because you're sailing into the westerlies. It had been considered almost impossible — Chay Blyth had done it but my boat was 20 feet smaller and yet I beat his record by 70-odd days. I was proud of that but I did it at the time of the Falklands War, when Pope John Paul II was visiting this country and Princess Diana was giving birth to Prince William, so there was virtually no coverage. But then there is very little flag waving even although that's not the reason for doing things. It's to deprive other nations of doing it first.'

A true circumnavigation is defined as passing through two antipodal points which are at least 12,429 statute miles apart. Blyth went round four capes but Scott Cowper took in five — Good Hope; Leeuwin; South East Cape, Tasmania; South West Cape, Stewart Island, New Zealand; and Horn.

The weather was three times as bad as previously and he was knocked down three times at Cape Horn and buffeted by winds of about 40 knots for two whole weeks. Waves were 60 feet high yet David insists his severest injury was housemaid's knee suffered during violent weather in the Tasman Sea when the huge waves tossed him into the air and he landed heavily.

He dismisses loneliness and fear as though they don't exist.

'I know that some people are lonely if they are left in an empty house for three days but I like my own company. I always have. It isn't a problem. And you never think of danger. It's always there — you can walk along a street and be mugged.

'People are always asking me if I worry about being ill on a voyage, of having a heart attack or toothache or things like that. But if you thought along those lines you would never do anything. Anyone can achieve anything they like if they put their mind to it. It's just that some people won't take the risk of untying the umbilical cord which attaches them to their home and a nine-to-five job.'

David, born during the Second World War in 1942, gained his love of sailing when he got into his father's small boat at the age of nine. Schooling took him to Aspatria in Cumberland and then Buckinghamshire though he adds significantly: 'I wasn't allowed to sail at school because I couldn't swim!'

By 1974 he had successfully competed in the *Observer* Round

Britain Race — a race for pairs — and two years later in the *Observer* Singlehanded Transatlantic Race.

'In 1979 I acquired my first boat which was built at Wallsend. I named it *Airedale,* not after the dog but after Lord Cardigan's yacht which he had at Balaclava because of my love of Crimean history. He used to entertain his mistresses aboard his boat though mine wasn't bought for the same reasons!'

Sailing in pairs, like the Round Britain Race, doesn't really appeal to the tall, balding Geordie with a dogged determination and an obsession with detail.

'I find going solo much better. Success is in the preparation and organisation. If your partner is not as fastidious as you are in cross-checking etc, then any expedition can flounder. You cannot accept things as being right, or leave it to someone else. Any voyage can go wrong because of something minuscule. I've got high standards and I expect them in others. Builders hate me — I check everything and can find the smallest fault which is usually made through speed.

'But then I feel the overall standard of general tradesmen has gone down. In the old days a person would spend three or four years as an apprentice and then emerge with a guild certificate in welding or whatever. He knew his trade inside out and couldn't be bettered. But today if you spend six weeks at a job shop you know all about boat building. It's a nonesense.'

Working alone is not just a matter of putting your life in your own hands for Scott Cowper. It's a financial necessity also for a uniquely successful sailor who has never enjoyed the huge sponsorship afforded Chay Blyth or had the personal millions which backed Richard Branson on his Atlantic crossing.

'I work on my boats to keep the cost down. If I had someone to help me it could cost £12 an hour, and if you're working on a shoestring that's a luxury. I wasn't particularly mechanically minded but one learns — you have to. I do rely on others for experience but in the main it comes down to me. Unless you have the backing of a multi-millionaire it's a matter of scrounging the whole of the time. Every single item needs sponsoring, and while some firms will help, other don't want to know.

'A boat is as sophisticated as an aircraft, certainly it's got more components than a car. Most items have to be either hand made or custom made. Very few can be bought off the shelf. You can buy an engine but it doesn't stop at that . . . you need oil coolers, exhausts, filters. All fittings must be insulated and the engine bedded down etc. That's a lot of man hours as well as expense. People don't realise where the time goes.'

Sailing is an expensive occupation. 'We operate on the tradition of the British muddling through with second-best while the French pour millions into sailing. It's always compromise or substitution. It does hold me back. My last boat, the *Mabel E. Holland*, is a typical example. It was a very cheap boat, purchased from the RNLI on being taken out of commision and hard work to sail. My accomodation consisted of just one bunk and a chart table. I was surrounded by 150 five-gallon containers of fuel while if the boat had been purpose-built it would have had a huge fuel tank. But to build a 45-footer today would cost £450,000.'

It was in the converted lifeboat that Scott Cowper achieved his latest miracle, punching his way through the treacherous North West Passage over the top of the world from the Atlantic to the Pacific via the Arctic. Four long years it took him but he emerged as the first Englishman to complete such a feat.

The search for a passage from Europe to the Far East through the ice-blocked water of arctic Canada has lured explorers ever since the sixteenth century. Only in 1906 was the feat finally achieved by Roald Amundsen. The search for the North West Passage has been linked with such names as Frobisher, Cook, the Franklin Expedition of 1845 (in which 134 men lost their lives), and Larsen in the twentieth century.

This new challenge through the 5,000-mile stretch of water that bounds the North Pole was to engulf his life for the longest ever period because of the repeated breaks forced upon him by the severest of weather.

The *Mabel*, 42 feet in length and powered by two 48 h.p. Gardner diesel engines, was built in 1957 but had been brought to the Tyne by David in 1983 to undergo a refit at Smiths Shiprepairers of North Shields.

On July 14, 1986 with the tall ships attracting thousands to the banks of the Tyne, the *Mabel* slipped out into the North Sea not to return again for four years. After calling in at a Scottish port for more fuel, Scott Cowper headed for Greenland and then westwards into the mouth of the North West Passage where he encountered ice for the first time. The *Mabel* nudged its way between towering icebergs and flat floes that had been broken off the Arctic ice cap by the summer sun, easing its way along the 'leads', narrow stretches of open water that split the pack ice. In navigation terms it was a nightmare. There is no guarantee that the lead you sail into won't be a dead end. If it is, you have to turn round and attempt another, trying to recall any that you might have entered unsuccessfully already. And while you are trying to thread your way through this sub-zero maze, you have to keep track of your position, which is not easy when the proximity of the Magnetic North Pole makes the compass useless and heavy summer fog sometimes prevents you from taking a bearing from the sun.

Scott Cowper described it as 'navigating by the seat of your pants' and relied on his inbuilt sense of direction and the ability to 'sniff out' the correct route. Long hours were spent steering the boat by hand, because automatic navigation systems rely on the compass. Sixteen hours at a stretch was the most he could manage, then he had to try and find shallow water, drop anchor, and snatch a few hours in the confine of his bunk. And all the time there was the constant risk of a hull-rupturing collision with a floe or being crushed between a couple of huge icebergs.

By August 31, six weeks after starting out, the *Mabel* was completely iced in at Fort Ross where she spent the winter in total darkness with temperatures reaching -60 degrees C. In May, 1987 Scott Cowper returned to inspect the boat, hiring two Eskimo guides, a sledge and two skidoos to take him across the ice-covered waters. No progress could be made so he returned to the UK. Three months later he received an urgent call from *Resolute*. The Ice Reconnaisance Patrol had spotted *Mabel*. The ice had melted and she was taking in water and listing. David returned to inspect her to find his supplies, clothing etc under water. He spent some weeks drying out and had some winching equipment flown from Edmonton in order to pull her onto the shore for the oncoming winter. No progress was made that year as the ice didn't break at all.

By now it was June, 1988 and David left Newcastle to prepare *Mabel* for a continuation of the transit but unfortunately a company from the south of England which had offered to help with the red tape involved in air freighting essential equipment for repairing the boat had let him down and the freight failed to arrive. There was no alternative but to return to England to obtain duplicate equipment.

They were frustrating times — an explorer temporarily beaten by the weather and lack of help. However, two months later Scott Cowper, determination again to the fore, once more returned to the High Arctic, taking with him three kitbags of equipment. *Mabel* was put back into the water, winching equipment having been flown out from Edmonton yet again. At last there was a break in the ice enabling him to cover 1,500 miles of the Passage but *Mabel* was leaking so, apart from the difficulties of navigation David was also having to pump out water.

He reached Inuvik on the Alaskan border just 500 miles from his goal but the winter was settling in and it was impossible to proceed further that year. It meant *Mabel* spending another winter iced up in the High Arctic.

June, 1989 and Scott Cowper left Newcastle with two heavy kitbags and one container of equipment required to repair her leaking hull. The ice had taken its toll. He spent five weeks alone carrying out repairs to *Mabel's* hull then sanding and painting her. Eventually Scott Cowper left Inuvik on July 28 with only 500 miles of ice to negotiate before reaching Point Barrow.

But he would have to negotiate some 1,500 miles of treacherous seaways before reaching Dutch Harbour in the Aleutians where he could rest and refuel. On August 16, 1989 Beryl Turner, his voyage co-ordinator and organiser, received a call from Dutch Harbour to say that David had made it and become the first Englishman to transit the North West Passage singlehanded.

His adventure was far from over, however. Many, many miles of sailing lay ahead of him. After a few days' rest he was on his way to Midway Island, a top-security U.S. navy missile base in the Pacific which requires permission from Washington for entry. At first this was refused, but with a little pressure from local MP Neville Trotter and the Admiral of the U.S. Navy in London, Washington changed their minds.

Scott Cowper arrived at Midway on September 1, rested for a few days, refuelled and was again on his way to Papua, New Guinea. It took him three weeks and he made Port Morseby on October 2. Darwin was to be the last port of call in 1989 and he docked on October 22, *Mabel* coming to rest in the boatyard where she spent some weeks during her first voyage round the world.

As the Indian Ocean was in the middle of the cyclone season, Scott Cowper came home to his desk in his Savile Row office and months of waiting impatiently for his last leg of a journey few of us would even dare to dream about. Being deskbound isn't an adventurer's idea of fun but in March, 1990 the action began again. He flew to Australia, boarded *Mabel*, and returned in triumph up the Tyne with the Gateshead Garden Festival in full flow.

It was August, 1990 and *Mabel* was home for the first time since July of 1986. The whole trip had cost him an awful lot of his own cash but the man alternatively called stubborn, patient, obsessed, heroic and foolhardy felt the deep glow of self-fulfilment.

He already had no fewer than 18 firsts entered in the *Guinness Book of Records*. Now there were more. But compare him with other greats and talk about camaraderie, about an elitist club sipping gin and tonics and swapping fascinating yarns of countless heroics, and he shakes his head.

'It's pretty rare for us to see each other. Chay Blyth is in Plymouth, I'm in Newcastle and Dame Naomi James . . . well, I don't even know where she is.

'We don't compare notes. There is a certain amount of competitive edge between us and that doesn't lend itself to a lot of fraternisation.'

As far as heroes go, Scott Cowper rates Sir Francis Chichester highly.

'Chichester was a great pioneer. In 1910 he flew *Gypsy Moth* round the world, which in those days was a considerable feat, and during the war he was responsible for designing bomber sites. He was a very capable individual in his own right. He hit sailing in the early 60's when it was taking off. It was a good time after the war when more cash was available and people had more leisure time.'

Scott Cowper admits that he's totally obsessed with sailing and sees Chichester as something of a reassurance against old age.

'He was 67 when he achieved his greatest feat, which shows that sailors can go on. Sitting in an old people's home with chairs round the wall of the television room is not my idea of fun. Age can be so cruel. I've got nothing else in my life but sailing. It's a selfish occupation, but then so are a lot of professions. I can go round a golf course when I'm 80 or 90. I don't want to do it now.'

David's idea of a holiday isn't to fly to Majorca on a package flight like so many Geordies. He doesn't particularly like the sun, preferring cooler conditions. No, for him the idea of total relaxation is to visit the west coast of Scotland and go sailing.

As with any adventurer in the final years of the twentieth century, new challenges become fewer and fewer. But Scott Cowper's next challenge is already in the pipeline.

'There's always the North East Passage. Like the North West Passage it's never been done single-handed before. The Norwegian Amundsen did it in 1917, I believe.'

Yes, but Amundsen had a little help in the form of a crew and a slightly larger boat!

# Miriam Stoppard

**IT WAS** Coronation Day 1937 and everyone was out on the streets celebrating. A savage war was about to engulf Europe and plunge us into darkness for six long years. Adolf Hitler was already mesmerising the German people with his hypnotic speeches. But on May 12, 1937 the whole nation was gripped by national fervour. George VI was being crowned and it was a time for joy.

Philip Street in Newcastle's west end was like every other street in the land. The occupants were outside toasting the king and having one huge party. But in an upstairs flat Jenny Stern was about to give birth to her first child. Home confinements were the general rule in those days, but getting hold of a doctor proved more than a little difficult in the circumstances.

One was eventually found, however, and Miriam was delivered. You could say she was born lucky — every child who came into this world on Coronation Day qualified for a £5 bounty. There were only two born in Newcastle and Miriam was one of them.

'The Lord Mayor of Newcastle presented us with our £5, a lot of money then, and we bought a pram with beautiful high wheels for four guineas,' recalls her proud mum. 'She was a very beautiful baby. A little queen, she was, very fat with rosy cheeks.'

Today that little girl has grown into an equally beautiful and brilliant lady, witty and wise . . . Miriam Stoppard, MB, BS, MD, MRCP. Doctor, TV personality, author, health adviser, mum. Married to famous playwright Tom Stoppard and decidedly happy with her lot.

She's now miles away (and years away) from Newcastle, a city she left at the age of 18, but she remains a fiercely loyal Geordie, protective of her upbringing and background.

'I think the Geordies are great; they're tenacious, they've a lot of grit and guts and at the same time they're very canny. I learned a lot being brought up a Geordie. It's just grit that got me where I am.'

Jenny and Sid Stern are Jews who ran a strictly Kosher household raising two brilliantly clever daughters, Miriam and Hazel who is two years younger. There were no comics allowed in the house. 'For all our elementary education we encouraged our daughters to read good books, the classical books,' said Sid. 'Miriam gets her intelligence from her mother. Although she left school at 14, Jenny is the clever one. By the time she was 18 she was a forewoman with Robert Sinclairs, the tobacco people.'

Miriam was a toddler, Hazel a babe in arms when war finally broke out. It meant automatic hardship, as it did for millions of families. Sid was called up straight away and Jenny and the girls were evacuated from Tyneside. Their furniture was put into storage and with 30 other families they were sent to the seaside village of Arnside on Morecambe Bay.

They were taken into the church hall with all the residents sitting around, deciding who they would take on. Gradually the families were selected until the Sterns were the only ones left. Someone said: 'Who will have a mother and two children?' and a school mistress, who was on the local committee, stepped forward. Ironically, within two weeks, the Sterns were the only family left. All the other mothers returned home because they were homesick.

Miriam's early childhood was spent as a wartime evacuee — 18 months at Arnside and the rest of the war nearer home at Bamburgh, a delightful village on the Northumberland coast where she started school. She loved it. Quick to learn, with an inquiring mind, her teacher called her 'a bright little light'.

Those times of adversity . . . dad away at the war writing religiously every day and the kids putting their little scribbles on mam's letters in return . . . were character building to a child with a basic determination.

'We had a hard life,' says Miriam, looking back with not a little affection. 'We were a poor family. Things were tough and I think it's an awfully good way to start life. It makes you resourceful and ingenious and determined. It tempers the steel. I'm a great believer in adversity.'

The war over, the Stern family moved back to Newcastle and Miriam continued her education at Wingrove Road Senior School in Fenham. Her determination to succeed was emphasised when she received her first school report. She was second out of a class of more than 30 children, something of which many would have been justifiably proud. Instead Miriam burst into tears. She wanted to be first!

It was a steeliness, the burning will to win and come out on top, that was to make Miriam Stoppard the highly successful businesswoman she is today. Not suprisingly, her last report from Wingrove School put her in first place out of a class of 34 with perfect marks in nearly every subject. Her form teacher wrote: 'Miriam has done excellent work throughout the term and should have a great future ahead of her in her new school.'

That was in 1948, the year Miriam was awarded a free scholarship to Newcastle's Central High School. There was no way her parents could have afforded to send her, of course. They were looking towards Rutherford School as her natural progression because school fees were out of the question. But she passed the two written exams and an oral examination to go to the Central High.

Once there she excelled across the board. It was, she says, a school which pushed you, though while she responded she found it hard and sometimes painful. She was fearful of failing and falling short of expectations. But she reponded to being pressurised, just as she has all of her life, and by the time she left in the summer of 1955 she had passed her A levels in four science subjects.

Her father helped by gently encouraging her ambition. 'I used to say to her: "Miriam, can you imagine yourself as a sister in a ward with all the nurses working under you?" Then she got her scholarship to Central High and I would say: "Miriam, can you imagine yourself as a matron in charge of all those sisters and nurses?" And when she started bringing in some of her reports, it was: "Miriam, wouldn't it be nice to be a doctor?" '

Miriam herself says: 'The most important lessons I learned from Central High, my parents, my Geordie background, and my wartime evacuation to Bamburgh and the Grace Darling Story, was the expectation of equality. You get what you expect and if you expect equality you get that. It means that I'm in the fortunate position of not needing women's lib.'

Hard work and no play can make more than Jack a dull boy, of course, and Miriam had her moments. Come Saturday and Sunday she put her books away and had fun at the local Maccabi youth club. 'Quite a few boys were after her,' remembers her mam with parental pride. She also represented her school at tennis, swimming and hockey.

Despite her upbringing Miriam, who continued her studies on a state scholarship at the University of London, never did marry a Jewish boy. Her first marriage to a Yorkshire vet ended in divorce — for a number of years she practised under her married name of Dr Miriam Moore-Robinson — and then in 1972 she married Tom Stoppard. There were no children from her first marriage but now with husband Tom she has two stepchildren (Oliver and Barnaby) and two of her own (William and Edmund).

Home is a country house in Buckinghamshire surrounded by four acres of land: 'My most cherished possession is my garden because it's the only reliable source of tranquility,' she says.

She worked in clinical medicine, specialising in dermatology, and joined the pharmaceutical industry, becoming Managing Director of the giant Syntex Pharmaceuticals Ltd, an international drug company based in California. She quit in 1980 because, she decided, 'I was taking out a great deal of care and affection from my family's bank of love for me and not paying back enough to them.'

But what really thrust Miriam Stoppard into the public eye was television, a medium for which she was a natural. As a presenter with Yorkshire Television's 'Don't Ask Me' science programme for children she was the beauty with brains who countered the outrageous masculine energies of Magnus Pyke and David Bellamy.

Other shows followed, notably 'Where There's Life' in which she made headlines by kissing an AIDS victim on the programme. In a few seconds she swept away the ignorance and fear about a disease which had hit the world with the impact of an atom bomb. It was the gesture of a warm and caring human being, not just of a doctor.

'I take my responsibilities on television even more seriously than I did when I was a doctor looking after thousands of patients. The studio audience and I are bound together and we all realise it.

'I would never criticise people, and those who ask how I persuade people to talk to me like they do should know there is no secret. All there is is the knowledge that they will not be judged. I would never say to anyone: "How could you?" What I may say is: "Tell us more."

'People learn most from hearing others describe what it's like to be at rock bottom — and how they can climb back up.'

Her celebrated interview with AIDS victim Amy Sloan was done in a workingmen's club after some technicians at Yorkshire Television had refused to work in the same place as the 24-year-old American sufferer.

'I did it spontaneously for a medical reason to dispel ignorance and fear and not as a stunt. We were having our photographs taken and Amy's cheek was right next to me and it seemed quite natural just to turn and give her a kiss.

'I don't want to bring about a revolution. I just want to bring about a shaft of light.'

Her rare ability to make people open their hearts as though they were having a cosy chat with a confidant away from the prying eye of the television camera touches even the famous. In 'Woman to Woman' Prime Minister Margaret Thatcher — the Iron Lady — was unexpectedly reduced to tears when talking about her father.

'I never expected her to say the things she did,' admitted Miriam. 'It was really revealing and very moving and explains so much about the way she is.'

Books, too, established the Miriam Stoppard reputation as the champion of women. She's written on babycare, the face and body, feeding your family, 50-plus lifestyle and sex among other things. And she's publicised great issues for women such as breast cancer.

She believes women put themselves down far too often and she encourages them to look at themselves in a new light. This may be the age of the liberated woman but deep down many still cling to outdated ideas.

'Women don't believe in themselves enough. Feeling good is half the battle. A woman who feels good can be in command of any situation. Women don't know how to accept compliments. You can say to them, "That's a nice dress" and they'll gasp, "Why, this old thing, I've had it for years" or "It cost £2.99 in a sale years ago." Why can't they just say "Thank you" and enjoy the confidence such a compliment should have given them?

'Most women see themselves as more overweight than they actually are. I know loads of men who think they're great but I don't know any women who think they're great. Ask a woman, "Do you like yourself?" and the answer is likely to be "No." What women have to do is say to themselves, "I really do like me — I think I'm great".'

She speaks with such conviction that you tend to forget that here is a pretty lady who has it made. She is a communicator, a convincer, someone who gives hope to others that they too can climb their personal Everest.

Her parents are now living in a house just a stone's throw away from their elder daughter. She persuaded them to leave Newcastle to be nearer her because family is the centre of her life despite her successes.

'I think I got the best of both of them. From my mother came energy, a constant desire to finish what I begin, and a great sense of optimism. And from my dad comes the determination and curiosity to find out, to delve into facts for their own sake. They're marvellous, marvellous people.

'Emotionally I'm very fulfilled. There is very little conflict in my life. If I had six months to live, then I wouldn't change a thing. I'm infinitely more in love with Tom now than when we married, but it's a love that's changed, as I think it must. When we first met and we used to go places, I was always down on the invitation as "guest." It was "Tom Stoppard and guest," and when people spoke to me — and they often didn't — and asked who I was, all I could say was that I'd come with Tom.

'Now I don't have to explain that but it just highlights how all the people who think I've had it easy, that I have never looked back, really don't understand. They can't appreciate how little we had when I was young, how we were shunned by many people because being Jewish at that time wasn't something to stand up and shout about. They don't, or wouldn't, believe the bad times I've come through — and don't think I don't consider I'm a lucky girl today. I can't forget where I came from and I thank God for the tough characteristics of the Geordie.

'My family are my No. 1 priority. Take away everything else and I still have enough.'

# John Hall

**WYNYARD HALL,** the magnificent stately home once owned by the Marquis of Londonderry, stands in 6,000 acres of rolling countryside in Cleveland. As you drive through the gates sheep are grazing contentedly in the grounds and pheasants walk proudly across the grass. Down the sweeping drive and over its famous bridge, and in front of you unfolds the hall itself, magnificent in its splendour and surrounded by a tranquil lake.

When I was first shown round it by a justifiably proud John Hall, he said: 'Not bad for a miner's son from Ashington, eh?' Not bad, not bad at all!

John and his wife Mae bought Wynyard Hall for £5m and are already well into a £300m plan which will see three golf courses designed by Tony Jacklin, an equestrian centre and a centre for music and the arts spring up creating between 10,000 and 15,000 jobs for the North East.

Hall, a fiercely proud Geordie born at North Seaton near Ashington, has risen from working at the local pit to a multi-millionaire with his company, Cameron Hall, which has business interests all over Europe.

It was he who built the MetroCentre at Gateshead on a 100-acre site of industrial waste and turned it into the most advanced retail/leisure complex in Europe, laying at the same time the foundation stone of his continued success. Yet he has never forgotten his roots. His best friend Gordon Proctor used to work with him at the pit and regularly jets out on Hall's private plane for a holiday at John's sumptuous house at Cascais, just along the coast from Portugal's capital city Lisbon. And Hall often entertains parties of miners or old folk from Ashington at Wynyard. He's the epitome of local boy makes good. A doer with a vast appetite for work.

His was not a privileged background but inside him burned ambition as brightly as any torch in the night sky. He was, recalls Mae who met him 38 years ago at Newcastle's Oxford Galleries dance hall, a young man going places. Someone always one step ahead who knew exactly where he was going.

He progressed very deliberately from his job as mines surveyor at the Lynemouth, Newbiggin and Ellington pits to being a chartered surveyor, taking charge of the Coal Board's farms at Ashington, and then assistant estates manager for the Northumberland County Council at Killingworth New Town before finally moving into his own development business.

'It was at Killingworth that I learned all about property development,' Hall told me. 'I was there four years but the ambition was always to get into private sector practice. I initially went into partnership in Sunderland where I spent another four years before setting up my own development company. I built that up — it was worth about £1.5m to £2m — but in 1974 the crash came and the NatWest Bank carried me through the next two years.

'We really took off around 1976 to 1978, and it was a year later when I looked over the fence on an October day on the Western Bypass at a waste tip that my dream of a shopping centre first dawned.'

That dream was to produce the MetroCentre and develop a company which today is worth between £80m and £100m — a staggeringly successful enterprise.

Yet Hall, an only child, was brought up in the shadow of the pit shaft at Ashington in an environment dominated by the National Union of Mineworkers and the Labour Party. When he left Bedlington Grammar School at 16 there were no jobs and he experienced the humiliation of being on the dole for six months before he and two friends found work with the National Coal Board as trainee surveyors. That was in 1949.

Those formative years of comparative hardship and blind loyalty to the Labour Party were to have a profound effect on John Hall and help fashion the future self-made millionaire. Yet they were happy times of childish pursuits and laughter.

'The men knew nothing but work and the welfare hall in

Ashington. Because of the difficult and varied shifts for pitmen there was no family life. I never saw my father during the week and Saturdays consisted of going to watch either Newcastle United or Ashington play football and doing shopping.

'My dad first took me to watch United when I was eight. We caught the No. 3 bus to Newcastle and went to the Co-op where my mother had a note — tick if you like — to get our clothes at the wholesale department. Then we'd have lunch at the Co-op and my dad would take me up to the match. We went in the Leazes end of the ground and if you were early you would get a place on the plank so you could see the match easily.

'After the game we would go down to the Haymarket where mam would be keeping our place in the bus queue. There were five cinemas in Ashington at the time and Saturday nights meant a visit to the pictures.

'On Sundays we would go to Whitley Bay and walk along the sea front, perhaps call into the Spanish City, and have high tea in one of the cafes. You know, fish and chips, tea, bread and butter.'

Sport figured highly in the life of the young John Hall. He played right-half or centre-half for his grammar school and later joined West Sleekburn Juniors. River fishing was his other activity though he'd occasionally take out a skip on the River Wansbeck. 'We held our own version of the Henley Regatta.'

Hall was brought up a staunch Labour man just like his father but, as an inquisitive mind began to query the poverty around him, he moved to the SDP and finally became a firm Thatcherite.

'Ashington folk in those days had limited experience of life though they were very good people. There was no money or cars or TV. Just community life built around the pits and the Labour Party. The miners had blind faith, the party could do no wrong. Towards the end my father was moved from pit to pit as a Labour Government closed them down but he wouldn't query what was happening. He worked 50 years down the mines from the age of 14 to 64 yet all he ended up with was a piece of paper thanking him and £12 a week. He died of cancer two years after retiring and my mother got £1 a week pension. That got me thinking.

'The pitmen were always talking about change. I used to go to meetings with my dad and listen to all these men talking about what they would and wouldn't do. It made a great impression on me. It taught me that I had a duty to work but that I didn't want to go down the pit. I figured that wasn't the way for me, that there must be a better way to fulfil that duty.'

Initially Hall spent six months cycling round Ashington looking for a job — a forerunner, perhaps of the famous 'on your bike' speech by Norman Tebbit to the unemployed — before his old headmaster at Bedlington Grammar School sent a message to Newbiggin Colliery recommending him.

'My father always said it was easier to get a job when you were in work. If you didn't like it you still had the experience. Training as a mining surveyor meant I was actually down the pit at the coalface three days a week and spent the other two days in the offices. I saw many a man killed at the pit face. It had a great effect on you.'

The Metro Centre dream was conceived in the late 1970's after many visits by John Hall to study out-of-town shopping centres in the United States and Canada. Such centres had been part of the retail scene since the 1950's and part of the normal way of life to the North American.

To Hall the advantage of these shopping centres was such that he couldn't see why the ideas could not be developed in the United Kingdom, but of course, the thinking by our planners and even the retailers was firmly wedded to keeping retail development in the city centre. In many instances the city fathers were partners in the vast redevelopments of city centres which had taken place in the 1950's and 60's. It was not in their interest to have out-of-town competition to their town-centre schemes.

It wasn't until the concept of the Enterprise Zone was first mooted by Mrs Thatcher and the Conservative Government in 1979 that it was possible to start thinking about changes in the pattern of retailing in the U.K. Enterprise Zones are areas which are generally free from planning restrictions and controls, which means that the brief for development is very wide indeed. It was in 1979 when the first Enterprise Zones were planned that John Hall's dream began to become a reality. The Tyneside Enterprise

Zone was designated in 1981 with its attractive package of tax benefits, freedom from rates and lack of planning restrictions for 10 years, and thus made his dream for an out-of-town shopping centre realistic.

Part of the zone was a huge 100-acre site lying between the motorway and the riverside. It was derelict, waterlogged, had been a tip for the local power station ash and was totally unsuitable for development without expenditure of vast sums of money to reclaim the land. It was a moonscape; but in his mind's eye he could see it all . . . Marks and Spencer over there, Carrefour on that site and half-a-dozen multiples along that mall with an exceptional standard of design and decor. He wanted to make it the best shopping centre in the western world.

However, it took some time to convince these retailers that Gateshead was the right place to be and it was not until 1984, when the final plans came to fruition and the scheme rapidly took place, that Marks and Spencer said they were going into the Centre. The scheme grew and grew until it reached its maximum size of 2 million square feet under one roof with 300 shops of all types, and a large fun fair. A place for meeting and socialising as well as shopping. A place where people could sit and watch the world go by, where old men would be able to meet up with their friends, a place with peaceful and tranquil corners for relaxation away from all the hustle and bustle.

There was still a lot of hustling to be done, however, like convincing the London financial houses that he had a winner. Investment in the North East was bad news to such people with its previous history of industrial decline, but finally Hall persuaded the banks that the MetroCentre was a magnificent possibility because of the benefits of the Enterprise Zone and the superb location of the site next to a major urban motorway.

Work had started in 1982 with the reclamation of the site, appointment of the main contractors, sinking the first steel and bringing together all the consultants and sub-contractors necessary to carry out the job and to put all the pieces of the jigsaw in place.

It was a team effort and finally in April 1986 stage one was opened. Stage two was trading by October 1986 and the third stage was completed and operational by October 1987 including the rail and bus stations. The whole centre is now well established and is operating successfully — very successfully. In 1989 nearly 20 million people visited the MetroCentre and spent £400m. They came from far and near and the centre enjoys tremendous support from places such as Scandinavia, Scotland, Holland and all parts of the North of England. It has been a success unparalleled in modern retailing and it has created 6,500 jobs for the people of the North East. Most of the £250 million cost was spent with firms in the region which helped many of these businesses.

Hall and the MetroCentre became examples of the kind of enterprise initiative the Thatcher government was encouraging.

From the dream to reality took 10 years, with a lot of heartaches in the beginning and a lot of smiles at the end. The risks for Hall and his family in the beginning were enormous, but with determination, and the backing of a very good team around them, they succeeded against all the odds.

The true success is that the MetroCentre is now a symbol of the revival and regeneration of the North East of England. It was all the sweeter when the American Institute of Shopping Centres recognised the quality of the development by awarding it the joint first prize at their 1989 conference in Las Vegas.

The scheme has been designed by people in the North East for people in the North East and has conclusively demonstrated to the world the talent amongst the local people. It has now become a major tourist attraction and continues to go from success to success, attracting ever-increasing numbers of shoppers and visitors.

Meanwhile Hall has moved on to other things and to development schemes in Europe, but the site of his next dream and ambition lies within his own region, the North East, at Wynyard Hall itself. He plans to turn it into Europe's largest leisure complex with three golf courses designed by Tony Jacklin, two hotels, leisure, function and conference facilities, 400 luxury houses, field sports and an equestrian centre, a centre for music and the arts, and a 400-acre business park. A £300 million investment, creating 10-15,000 jobs — the North East's next growth point.

Hall talks quickly, like a machine gun rat-tat-tatting out its message. The overwhelming impression is that time is precious, and that there is much to do every day. I've sat with him in a meeting where accountants have been walking in and out dealing with the intricacies of Newcastle United's share plans, his secretary Hazel has been repeatedly seeking guidance on a guest list and speeches for a large Wynyard Hall dinner, and the Mayor has just arrived for a separate function. But Hall is an expert juggler, his astute mind switching easily from one subject to another and back again without the flicker of an eye.

His work rate and his itinerary are phenomenal and he overlords everything even though his wife Mae contributes significantly, his son Douglas is managing director of Cameron Hall and his daughter Allison also works for the company. Mae, in fact, is very much part of the Hall team. A strong-willed lady with an engaging personality, she helped John to get the bandwagon rolling and he never underestimates her advice. Indeed she is the Cameron in the company Cameron Hall.

As an entrepreneur it's hardly surprising that Hall is a Thatcher man. He's had the Prime Minister visit the MetroCentre and counts among his personal friends the Conservative Party chairman Kenneth Baker. Yet while Hall lives in luxury and flies round the world in his private jet expanding his empire, he remains a man with the common touch. When I flew to his villa in Portugal with him for a week's break he took along his friend Gordon, who had begun work with him at the pits. They are still very close despite what John has gone on to achieve.

Mind you, while we were lounging round his swimming pool and basking in the sun, Hall was down at his office in Cascais every day and constantly on the phone taking calls from England. If he attempted to sit for more than five minutes, he was fidgeting as though he was wasting time.

But every man needs relaxation. Work may even become play, days run into nights, but sometime, somewhere must come a natural break. For John Hall in Portugal that meant, late at night after dinner, putting on a video of a live Tina Turner concert. It was a different side of the man, pin-striped suit and business rat-tat-tat gone. Instead we saw a laughing fan letting his hair down as the raunchy rock star belted out her most famous songs. It was sheer heaven for me, an equally committed Tina Turner fanatic.

Yet somehow, surprising as it may have seemed to see a successful man reduced to the role of enthusiastic fan, it was appropriate. She sang with vigour and verve, throwing herself into every number, never relaxing for a moment with a quiet song. Here was the same pace as John Hall lives his life. In a way strange but kindred spirits.

His high-profile battle with Newcastle United — 'Geordies should have a say in the running of the club' — took a lot of courage. The flak and dirty tricks brigade was almost a daily occurrence yet only served to intensify his determination to succeed.

The idea of standing up on behalf of the fans and demanding a share issue to democratise the club and weaken the stranglehold of an intransigent board of directors was born out of the frustration which also poured down from the terraces. Hall had a luxury box at St. James's Park and stood as a catalyst for other box owners sickened by the fact that United hadn't won a domestic trophy for more than 30 years despite a huge loyal following.

He formed the Magpie Group but really Hall was the only driving force. He put his money where his mouth was and entered into a buying campaign against the board to give him some power. In the end £1 shares in the club were going for £3,500 as the board continually bid against Hall. He sought change, not a takeover, but in the bloody war which ensued he bought out two directors, George Dickson and Ron Mckenzie, making them instant half-millionaires, and forced United to the negotiating table. This was a man who doesn't lose a battle he enters but who was originally severely underestimated by those opposing him.

To the fans he was a knight in shining white armour but he played his cards astutely rather than weighing in with bravado. 'There is more than one way to skin a cat,' he would tell the less patient amongst his supporters, and so it turned out.

It was perhaps appropriate that Hall, a highly successful businessman, should become a director of the football club he has supported since being a lad of eight.

Pointing to his nose, he smilingly told me: 'That's what Newcastle United gave me! I played at St. James's Park once, for East Northumberland against N's, Newcastle nursery team which was outstanding at the time. A ball was played over my head, I turned quickly, and whack . . . I ran straight into Tot Smith, a giant of a centre-half who broke my nose. I guess I've put one or two other people's nose out of joint at St. James's since!'

Inside a week in April of 1990 Hall's two-year battle with Newcastle United ended with him joining the board, and he flew by Concorde to America to be honoured by Yale University. They made him a Gordon Grand Fellow, reserved for 'outstanding figures in the world of business, industry and finance', an accolade bestowed in the past on the likes of David Rockefeller, the Chairman of the Chase Manhatten Bank; Gordon Getty III, Director of the Getty Oil Company; Roberto Goizueta, Chairman and Chief Executive of the Coca Cola Company; and Victor Kiam II, Chairman and Chief Executive of Remington Products Inc.

In honouring a Briton, Yale University broke new ground. But then John Hall has never known any boundaries.

# Brendan Foster and Steve Cram

**ARGUABLY** Brendan Foster has almost achieved as much in athletics since leaving the track as he did when he ran, head rolling and face grimacing, round Grystal Palace. Which is saying quite a lot when you consider his achievements as Britain's No. 1 distance man.

Big Bren was a star before the door was officially opened to monetary gain and full-time athletes. He originally worked as a schoolteacher in Hebburn and ran out of pride in the vest with no sack of gold at the end of the rainbow. Expenses on the train from Newcastle to London for the big meets were the official thank you. None of the five-figure appearance money for the Pied Piper of the British track who, in eleven years at the top from 1970, won one Olympic bronze medal, one gold and one bronze in the European Championships, three Europa victories, five AAA titles, and one gold, one silver and two bronze in the Commonwealth Games as well as setting two world records. He retired a Member of the British Empire, Bachelor of Science and Master of Athletics.

That in a nutshell was the running career of Foster but, like all facts and figures, it doesn't tell the full story. Putting the flesh on the bones gives a much more rounded view of an athlete who dragged the North East into the international spotlight it had never previously enjoyed. Sure, many moons ago Alec Burns and Jack Potts had left Tyneside to run in the Olympics of the early thirties (without winning medals) and Morpeth Harrier Jim Alder had won the Commonwealth Games marathon in 1966 (as a Scot!), but it was Foster, born in Hebburn by the Tyne, who propelled us permanently into the world scene.

Though he ran in the 1972 Olympic Games over 1,500 metres — I was in the magnificent Munich Stadium to watch him in the final — it was over 5,000 and 10,000 metres that he excelled to become a household name.

When I asked him a decade later to cast his mind back and select his finest hour there was no hesitation.

'Oh, my 5,000 metres gold medal in the European championships of 1974 without question,' he told me. 'I'd just set a world time for the 3,000 metres at Gateshead a couple of weeks before and I was really feeling good. I didn't want to just win the gold but to do it in style in the way Zatopek and Kuts had done it before me.

'Most 5,000 metres races are won in a sprint over the last lap but I thought, damn it, I'm going to go out and bomb. The temperature was 90 degrees but I led from the start and won with the field trailing way behind me. I clocked 13 minutes 17 seconds which was good. Only three or four, including myself, had ever ran faster and it was a better time than the 1990 Commonwealth Games 5,000 was won in 16 years later.

'That is the victory for which I'm remembered more than any other. If ever I meet an Italian, even today, they'll automatically say "Roma, Roma" with a big smile on their face. It's obviously stuck in the memory.'

An Olympic bronze over 10,000 metres in Montreal two years later was no mean feat, either, when it's remembered that Foster was our only track and field medallist that time round.

'At the time you probably feel like throwing it in the river because it's not gold but then you get a sense of proportion. It becomes a valuable part of your collection. I'm certain Steve Cram felt exactly the same way.'

Lasse Viren, the flying Finn with the Midas touch, haunted Bren. Gaunt, with a mystique which fascinated the average sports fan, he only beat Foster three times in his entire career but each time was a hammer blow in the biggest races of all, the Olympics. Viren's ability to 'disappear' for four years then emerge as a wonder runner at the Olympics brought synical accusations of blood doping but the big Geordie refuses to tarnish the reputation of an athlete he still reveres. He was, says Foster, 'the greatest runner of my generation.'

'Viren was a man apart in Montreal. Apart from winning the 10,000 when I got my bronze medal he also took the 5,000 when I was fifth. Then on the Sunday after the 5,000 final he ran the marathon. I was so stiff I could hardly move yet here was an athlete pushing his body almost beyond endurance.'

Lasse fully recognised the ability of the Briton who could be his master on any track in the world away from the Olympic flag, and after trailing in third in that epic European Championship run under the relentless sun of Rome he hailed Foster's golden victory as 'the greatest performance I've seen.'

Official recognition of Big Bren's Roman holiday and his world record came when he was voted BBC Sportsman of the Year, beating world champion boxer John Conteh and world racing driver James Hunt.

Throughout the seventies Brendan was Britain's No. 1, the undisputed king of the track over the longer distances. Not once, in all that time, did a Briton head him in a major championship. He had his rivals, his head to heads with the likes of fellow Geordie Mick McLeod and Ian Stewart, but it was Foster who was the boss.

'I think Mick only beat me a couple of times and then not in the major meets. Once was at Gateshead over 3,000 metres in 1978 which caused a bit of a flurry but, apart from being the organiser of the meeting with all that entails, I'd ran 200 metres against Geoff Capes in a fun race on the same night!'

There is no bitterness that Foster's glory years came before the big money which is now part and parcel of athletics and has been enjoyed by his good pal Steve Cram.

'When I was at the top I always had a daytime job and would train early in the morning before going to work and again at teatime when I'd finished. But, frankly, there was enough pressure without me running for a living. I preferred to run a few good races but if cash had been on the line I might have been forced into meetings where I wasn't keen to take part.

'No, I have no regrets. But I agree with athletes being paid as entertainers though I don't think it has been done awfully well. I remember going to London for the AAA Championships and in the *Radio Times* there were two pictures of me and Ian Stewart. It was billed as the great clash and there was I paying my train fare down to entertain thousands of fans and getting nowt. Somehow that never seemed fair.'

Foster's love affair with the Crystal Palace crowd, which was to be a feature whenever he ran there in televised races, began by accident.

'It came about in 1973 when I was teaching at the same school in Hebburn I'd attended as a kid. The PE teachers, George Felton and Mrs Coyle, organised a trip to London with some of the pupils to watch me run and, with plenty of advance planning, they had the best seats in the house just on the finish line. After I'd won the 5,000 metres I spotted them in the crowd and went over to give them a wave. The next thing I knew the crowd round them were waving and applauding and so it went on. After that I had to do the same thing every time I won there. It was expected of me.'

If Foster was a world-class athlete, then his vision as an administrator was unique. As the recreation officer for Gateshead Council he turned the town into an athletics hotbed. Years ago we had a glimpse of the stars when the likes of world mile record holder Derek Ibbotson came to Hebburn to run in a one-off race at a local works meeting. But under Bren's influence and pulling power Gateshead was to become established as an athletics centre of international stature.

Foster's invitation races — always superior to meaningless internationals in my mind — brought the world's best athletes to a town previously known in sporting circles for once losing a Football League club. Ed Moses, John Walker, Rod Dixon, Lasse Viren, Mary Decker, Seb Coe, Steve Ovett, Henry Rono, Don Quarrie . . . all came for the head-to-head races with the crowds pouring in. Big Bren was indeed the Pied Piper and Gateshead, with their reputation now firmly established on the world scene, went on from strength to strength after he left, finally winning the Europa Cup finals of 1989.

Foster also dreamed up the Great North Run — a fun run for 30,000 Geordies and exiles with a liberal sprinkling of world stars at its head.

'It was never a deliberate plan, more a stupid idea which came to glorious fruition. I mean, who would set out to stage the biggest race in Europe with 30,000 runners streaming over the Tyne Bridge on a Sunday morning?

'The thought first dawned on me when I was in New Zealand with David Moorcroft in 1980 to run in Auckland. We were asked to take part in a 10 kilometre race round the bay and when we turned up we couldn't believe it. The streets were packed with people and kids on roller skates, bikes, the lot were taking part. We were running along when suddenly someone would whizz past you on a skateboard. It was crazy but it got me thinking and by June of the following year the Great North Run was born.'

That Run has now developed into the Great North Festival of Sport while Foster has also been responsible for the televised City Centre Road Races and the international cross country meet in Durham at the end of each year.

I've had a good working relationship with Bren from his days as a runner, through Gateshead Rec, and on to Nike and finally his own company Nova International. He's sociable, with a wicked sense of humour, but beneath the surface lies a vision few are blessed with and the shrewdness of a politician.

He's still very much a public figure through his job as a BBC athletics commentator though he admits: 'While I'm in a privileged position I would much rather be remembered for what I achieved on the track than anything else . . . for how I did it, for the titles I won and the opposition I beat. I tried to be the best in the world on the track but I've never tried it in other things. My entry in *Who's Who* this year was changed from "athlete" to "athletics commentator". That's bad news.'

Bren is now the Beeb's right hand man to David Coleman — 'a true professional' — and as such has become a natural target for the famous Colemanballs. Something which appeals to his sense of fun.

'My first entry came after I was commentating on a meeting in Athens in 1982. We were going out live and there were three false starts in the women's 200 metres. David Coleman was obviously running out of things to say so he asked my opinion on the race. "Oh, I really fancy Kathy Cook," I said blithly!

'It was Kathy again who was the subject of another out take featured on the BBC review of the year. She was by far our greatest medallist and during the 1987 World Championships I innocently said: "It's a great shame Kathy Cook has given up the game." Almost immediately I realised the implications and doubled up with laughter. I couldn't help it.'

Foster and Cram are great mates. Both have a deep love and understanding of athletics at world level, both like a leg pull, and both are committed soccer fanatics — that's where they differ. Bren is a Newcastle United man. He has a private box at St. James's Park and says, without the flicker of an eye, that his greatest sporting dream was always to play centre-forward for the black and whites. Steve is a Sunderland diehard who regularly, during the winter cross-country season or at road races, has a car standing by to whisk him to Roker Park on a Saturday within minutes of him finishing.

Foster has actually worn the black and white stripes of United at Wembley . . . before the 1974 F.A. Cup final.

'I was first approached by the Football Association to run round the Wembley track prior to the 1973 final between Sunderland and Leeds United but I told them they must be kidding. Me supporting Sunderland! But a year later the F.A. came back when United made the final. I didn't fancy being a warm-up act but I said I'd do it if they gave me a dozen tickets for the match. They did and my dad, two brothers and my mates all had seats in the stand.

'It was a great feeling racing at Wembley with thousands of Newcastle supporters chanting "Foster is a Geordie." And I won, too.'

Bren, whose crown was to be so magnificently worn by the younger Cram, was directly responsible for the youngster's emergence onto the international scene.

'It came about when we both ran in the Emsley Carr Mile back in 1978. Crammy was still a teenager who had never worn an England vest and he finished fourth to my third. I only beat him because he was a kid from round the corner and my pride wouldn't let him get in front on the line. Two athletes had already been pre-selected for the 1,500 metres at the Commonwealth Games in Edmonton and my third place guaranteed me the extra place.

'But I was already booked for the 5,000 and 10,000 metres so I asked Steve if he fancied going to Canada in the 1,500. He nodded, wide-eyed, and I found Andy Norman and told him he must get Cram selected ahead of me. "We'll look after him in Edmonton," I assured Andy who promptly got two England selectors out of the stand and the deal was done.'

Cram's time in the Emsley Carr Mile was 3 minutes 57.04 seconds, the same as Foster. But what was significant, apart from the fact that he'd broken the four-minute barrier for the first time, was that he had also broken the world record for a 17-year-old which stood at 3:59 dead set by the legendary Jim Ryun.

Steve, like Bren born on the Tyne's banks, was on his way to fame and fortune; an athlete destined to smash the dominance of Seb Coe and Steve Ovett and open up another chapter in the glorious history of Brits in athletics' blue riband event.

Foster sums up the awesome ability of Cram in a couple of sentences. 'If no one was allowed to train he would be the greatest athlete ever to have lived. He's an absolute natural.'

As it is, Cram has secured his place in athletics' hall of fame — World 1,500 metres champion in 1983, European and Commonwealth 1,500 metres gold medallist in 1982 and 1986, Commonwealth 800 metres champion 1986 and Olympic silver medallist over 1,500 metres in 1984. That adds up to being a champion at every conceivable level outside the Olympic Games where he has finished second.

Such was the power, speed and stamina of Cram that in a matter of 19 days during the summer of 1985 he smashed no fewer than three world records at 1,500 metres, one mile and 2,000 metres.

Unquestionably of all the jewels in Cram's crown pride of place must be in winning the 1,500 at the inaugural World Championships in Helsinki. Previously the Olympic Games had been athletics' showcase but while the magic remained, political boycotts had diminished their stature; simply the world's best runners were not always there. There were to be no such boycotts in Finland. The gauntlet had been thrown down and Cram faced the cream in competition . . . Steve Ovett, the undoubted favourite, American Steve Scott who was also ahead of Cram in the betting, Said Aouita who had run the fastest time in the world that year, the highly experienced Mike Boit and Olympic champion John Walker.

Scott was the man who preoccupied Cram the most though the British were naturally building up the confrontation with Ovett. However, in the heats and semis Aouita had emerged as a growing threat and Brendan Foster, covering the championships for the BBC, tipped off Steve that the Moroccan planned to go from 500 metres out. Foster knew Aouita better than most and also knew his coach Carlo Grippo and realised what their race plan was. It was to prove decisive.

The race itself began like a funeral march. The runners went through 400 metres in a fraction under 65 seconds, slower than the women had run less than half an hour earlier. Cram would have preferred it faster to take the sting out of Ovett but he was boxed in near the back with Mike Boit. Coming up to two laps to go Cram began to move from his position on the inside. Past Scott, past Ovett, towards Aouita who was well positioned in fourth place as they entered the back straight. Jan Kubista was picking up the pace from the head, while Cram was immaculately placed out wide in the slipstream of Aouita.

The race was really on from about 800 metres. On the bend before the bell it was Kubista, Aouita, Cram and Scott, each on the other's shoulder waiting for the strike. Boit had come wide into lane three while Ovett was boxed on the inside last but one. Sure enough, Aouitas went at 500 metres, just as Foster had forecast.

Cram recalls: 'Aouita was flying now and everyone was stretched out. We had made the initial kick and gone up a gear. Now I was waiting for the big kick to come. At 300 Aouita went again and stretched us a little bit more. I wasn't even aware of anything else, hardly even who the runners were. I'd settled into the new kick and was ready to make my effort. I thought Aouita was beginning to die so I went for it. That was probably what won me the race.'

Foster maintained: 'The 200 mark was where Crammy really showed his class. He thought here's a chance, this guy's beginning to fade. If I wait till the straight there's going to be a queue of them ready to rush past me. So let's go for it now. So he went and that was it. The race might as well have stopped half way round the bend because Crammy had won it by then.'

Scott took the silver medal behind Cram with Aouita third and Ovett, who had run a stinking race tactically, back in fourth place out of the medals.

A year later came the next hype, the Olympic Games in LA. Seb Coe had seen his last two years ruined by illness and injury and was a world-class athlete who had suddenly become an unknown quantity, but what the public at large didn't fully realise was that the new world champion was equally badly prepared.

'A different type of athlete to myself wouldn't have gone,' says Cram now, with things having been put into perspective by the passing of time. 'Certainly with only four weeks to go to the Olympics I didn't think I was going. I'd suffered a groin injury and then a mysterious foot injury which came out of nothing and then, after three or four weeks, suddenly disappeared for no reason.

'It was a private time trial I ran at my own track in Jarrow that encouraged me — and Bren was a big help. He steadied me, made me take things easy in training instead of trying to whack in the mileage. But if someone had told me the gold medal would be won in 3 mins 32.53 secs I'd have stayed at home.'

This was one of the rare races when Coe, Cram and Ovett were in the same field, though illness was to reduce Ovett to a pale shadow of his former self. The final was quick right from the off. Omar Khalifa took the field through the first lap in 58.85 and Steve Scott kept the pace building to 1:56.81 after 800 metres. Coe had never been far from the leader while Cram was in close contention in fifth. But he was tiring.

Jose Abascal took up the running with 600 to go and as they approached the bell Cram's supporters were waiting for him to begin his long-sustained surge for home. Cram battled to get onto Coe's shoulder but the Olympic champ held off Steve's challenge on the last bend as they both left Abascal behind. Suddenly Coe hit the accelerator to power away with Cram's head rocking and rolling, and it was all over in a new Olympic record time.

'I'd lost to a stronger man on the day but I'd given more than 100 per cent so I couldn't be too disappointed. Three or four weeks later I was in great shape but that's the way it goes in athletics.'

Only the Olympic gold has escaped the giant Geordie yet he can smile at how close he's come to completing his set of winner's medals.

'People look back at '84 as my Olympic year with a silver medal, yet in '88 in Seoul I should have won it. I was officially ranked No. 1 in the world and was flying until I was unexpectedly struck down with injury in Italy 20 days before the Olympics. It meant that for the first time I was going into a big meet with no confidence and for once I felt the pressure. Yet I finished fourth two and half yards behind the winner while I was 10 yards behind Coe when I got my silver in '84. I was two hundredths of a second off a bronze medal, nine hundredths off the silver and three tenths off the gold.'

Cram gained a certain amount of revenge over Coe for the Olympic defeat when he beat him in Stuttgart in 1986 to take the European Championship 1,500 metres gold medal just a month after his double gold at 800 metres and 1,500 metres in the Commonwealth Games in Edinburgh.

Yet it's that 800 win, plus a comparatively obscure 1,000 metres victory at Gateshead, which still hold a cherished place in a bank of wonderful memories.

'It may sound like blowing my own trumpet but I would have stuffed anyone that day in the Commonwealth 800. A top-class athlete knows instinctively when he's right and I was spot on. I did 1:43.1 which is still the UK all-comers record and I've never really seen myself as a half miler.

'The other race which, looking back, gives me most satisfaction was over 1,000 metres at Gateshead in 1985. I'd just taken three world records in 19 days and was going for a fourth in what was probably the hardest of the lot. I was at home and that meant a lot — but it also meant a typical North East night with a near gale blowing off the Tyne.

'It was so bad I asked the organisers to put back my race. There was no one else of quality in the field — just pacemakers — but the noise in the home straight was deafening. I was shot but they kept me going and I almost did it. It would have been lovely but the way the crowd lifted me has stayed as a particular memory — aye, more than when I beat Seb Coe over 800 at Gateshead.'

Crammy always remembers his friends. I attended a party in a Jarrow social club when he got engaged to Karen Waters and on Saturday, December 17, 1983 was boogie-ing away at the Newcastle Moat House on the Coast Road after Karen and Steve had tied the knot.

A few years later when I accidentally bumped into him and his big mate Dave Roberts (best man at his wedding) in the Bigg Market and downed a considerable number of white wines, Crammy drove me home to Wallsend because I'd enjoyed a few too many — and then pranged his own car into a lamp post on his way home. What a thank you, eh?

Mind you, he was only returning a favour. A short while before I'd invited Steve to one of our Footballer of the Month awards for the players of Newcastle United and Sunderland. We use a restaurant in Jesmond Dene in Newcastle and the lunches normally last anything up to four hours as the banter flows freely. On this occasion we hardly noticed as the snow came down steadily throughout the proceedings — until we went outside and found ourselves almost knee deep in the white fluffy stuff.

We had to literally dig ourselves out of the Dene only to find there was chaos on the roads with the traffic reduced to a bumper-to-bumper crawl. The original plan was to drop Crammy off at home and both of us were then going to get changed into evening suits complete with dicky bow ties to go through to Durham where Steve was to receive a Sportsman of the Year award from Vaux Breweries. But it soon became obvious that, with all the chaos, time was running out and we rapidly changed our plans and headed straight for Durham.

When we eventually got there a couple of hours later Crammy was still in his ordinary gear while the rest of the guests were resplendent in black evening suits. It was a dilemma, with Cram the guest of honour, but all wasn't lost. We sorted out a waiter who was about the same size as Steve and headed for the toilet. The outcome was that Crammy received his award in the waiter's suit and black tie while the waiter served the meal in Steve's everyday clothes!

I'd first come across Steve when he was a bairn . . . lanky as a beanpole with a shock of wavy blond hair. I went to his mam and dad's house in Hebburn to present him with a Performance of the Month award, never realising that the same scrawny youth would grow up into one of the world's greatest 1,500 metres men.

His humour is infectious. To this day if you phone up his flat on the Quayside, where he plays snooker with his mates, Crammy will be on the answer phone speaking in Pakistani or Chinese.

And I shared one of my most unusual moments with him and Brendan Foster. I've done chat shows with international sporting celebrities all over the North East but the one we did together in a Durham jail beat the lot. We were searched on the way in and did the show in the chapel especially converted for the occasion. There were as many warders round the walls as prisoners sitting in orderly rows in front of us — men from all over the country — but Cram and Foster laughed and joked their way through the session as though they were at a Buckingham Palace garden party.

Afterwards all the prisoners lined up and filed past us to shake each of us by the hand. Foster and Cram may have run all over the world, but I reckon they have never had a more captive audience!

# Rowan Atkinson

ANYONE who has seen 'Blackadder' or 'Not The Nine O'Clock News' knows the comic genius of Rowan Atkinson . . . witty, irreverent, with a sharp cutting edge and, in the beginning certainly, a trifle adolescent. An appeal which especially captivates the under-35's.

Much of his talent lies in his wildly funny facial expressions, his brilliant timing, and his unerringly accurate observations of human mannerisms. Those large soulful eyes and rubbery face have become the tools of his trade.

Science's loss is very much entertainment's gain. He's knee-deep in awards and justifiably so as one of our most zanily brilliant young comics.

Perhaps his impact, at least on the theatrical scene, is not surprising, for Rowan Atkinson was born on Twelfth Night (January 6, 1955). Not into a theatrical family, I hasten to add, but as the third son of a farmer, Eric, and his wife Ella. His birth certificate shows his birthplace as Gosforth but Rowan suggests, in the interests of accuracy, that Jesmond may be more precise. 'The nursing home was, I believe, along Jesmond Road where the motorway now is.' No matter, the first 17 years of his life were spent at Consett before moving with his parents and brothers Rodney and Rupert to a farm at Stocksfield along the River Tyne. His father died not so long ago but his mother still lives in the village. His academic life was fashioned at the Choristers' School in Durham and then St. Bees in Cumbria before he moved on to Newcastle University where he took his first degree in electrical engineering before going to Oxford to research for his M.Sc.

His earliest recollections of a fascination with the stage go back to his primary school days in Stocksfield. He played the part of a peddler in 'The Old Woman Who Lived In A Shoe' at the Stocksfield Church Hall.

It was at the Theatre Royal in Newcastle that the young Rowan had his first taste of live theatre. 'Pantomime it would have been when I was ten or eleven. I remember feeling I was a bit old for it even then. It was Terry Scott, and when I bumped into him while I was doing my one-man show in Bath a couple of years ago I told him of my memories of him. He was still playing the same part, I think.'

It wasn't long after this 1960's encounter that Atkinson 'was doing something amusing for the audience of other schoolfriends in the changing rooms at my Durham school. I can't for the life of me remember what it was but it came as something of a surprise to me to discover that I, too, might be amusing. It was probably the last time that I went out to entertain in private.'

Rowan, like a lot of comedians, is a very private person. It is, he concedes, very difficult to be constantly polite to fans who demand that he be witty on the spot, be it in the street, in the supermarket, or wherever. Under the lights the performer emerges, outrageous with an acerbic wit, but it hides the real man . . . courteous, quiet-spoken and rather shy.

'I had a part in Bernard Shaw's 'St Joan' at the choir school and took part in lots of plays at St. Bees before spending three years at Newcastle University where I was awarded an Upper Second. I wasn't a terribly exciting student. I lived in a hall of residence — Henderson Hall — for all my time there and I worked very hard for that degree. I did some revues at Newcastle but they weren't very good ones really. They consisted mainly of 'Monty Python' rewrites as I recall.'

It was as a post-graduate at Oxford that the serious student finally gave way to the entertainer.

'It took me three years to get my M.Sc. — it should have taken me two. But I knew one year into Oxford that I was going to go into show business. I had an agent by the end of 1976.'

He met his writing partner Richard Curtis at Oxford and appeared in the sort of topical, satirical sketches that Oxbridge has made its speciality. University reviews were followed by stage appearances at Hampstead and in the Edinburgh Festival Fringe where his performances delighted audiences and critics alike.

It was while at Hampstead in the summer of 1978 that one critic hailed him as 'the funniest graduate clown since Jonathan Miller?'

Not surprisingly the man who made him laugh the most at the time was the brilliant John Cleese from the previous generation of scholastic talent. So perhaps it was fitting that while at Oxford his talent should come to the attention of three men who had earlier worked on the team that had given Cleese his first radio success in 'I'm Sorry I'll Read That Again'. He did four radio shows for David Hatch but has done none since. 'Radio was not my forte. I felt I had to be seen. I'm a visual comic.'

John Lloyd, who had become head of BBC radio light entertainment was eventually beaten in the race to secure Atkinson's budding genius by London Weekend Television's head of comedy Humphrey Barclay. Through Barclay, Atkinson made his TV debut in a big way while still at Oxford — a comedy play, 'Canned Laughter', penned by Rowan and Richard Curtis, and featuring Atkinson in all three lead parts.

'They offered me a series after that but I turned it down. 'Canned Laughter' was quite good as a debut but it showed my inexperience in TV. I was too young to carry a whole show on my own.'

Rowan's major breakthrough came in 1979, and while he may look upon 'Canned Laughter' as showing his lack of TV experience, others viewed it differently. A year later and Atkinson had switched channels to the BBC and true fame was just round the corner. John Lloyd recruited him for the team he was putting together for 'Not The Nine O'Clock News', a worthy successor to 'Monty Python' and the Cook and Moore shows of the 60's. His co-stars were Pamela Stephenson, all blonde and boobs and outrageous lines; Mel Smith, whose huge moon-shaped face and chubby exterior brings mirth quickly to the surface; and Griff Rhys-Jones, a great foil for Mel as shown later in their hiliarious 'Alas Smith and Jones' series.

It was a show of the 80's, full of sharp humour and shocks with the expressive Atkinson far and away the star who outshone the others. It brought him the BBC TV Personality of the Year award and thrust him very much into the public eye.

'I can honestly say that if I had chosen the other three myself I would have chosen the same people. John Lloyd actually brought us together but we had all heard of each other and liked what each other was doing. We had very different backgrounds, of course, and it took a little time to get the chemistry working properly, to dovetail as we would want. It was thc sccond series before we were totally satisfied, just as it was with 'Blackadder.''

Rowan and Richard Curtis did a lot of the early writing with Mel Smith contributing a little and freelance writers weighing in as well but by the end of the input of Griff Rhys-Jones had become a significant factor.

'We obviously got some complaints about our material being too rude but I didn't mind how rude we were as long as we were rude and funny. We were never gratuitously rude and a lot of stuff was rejected as being too obscene.'

'Blackadder' was born in 1983, a different vehicle to 'Not The Nine O'Clock News' but still carrying the unmistakable Atkinson stamp of zany humour. The first series was set in 1480 with Rowan playing Edmund, Duke of Edinburgh, alias Blackadder, the second son of a mythical Richard IV, played by Brian Blessed. He was an evil, sallow and embittered creature cursed by a deformed haircut, wrapped in a shapeless black riding cloak and sporting a particularly fatuous pair of shoes. Perfect for Atkinson's facial contortions, a cult figure with the tights of Errol Flynn and the hobbies of Edward II.

Rowan, once again co-writer with Curtis, turned his eyes homeward for inspiration to Alnwick Castle, so loved by film-makers. Yet, though it won Atkinson an International Emmy, television's equivalent to the Oscar, in America it didn't totally please a perfectionist.

'It wasn't good value,' insisted Atkinson with a frankness not usually associated with the usual actor's ego. 'It had its moments but, God knows, there weren't enough of them and we didn't give enough reason for laughing at the character. It was also a very expensive series. When you take 12 horses up to Alnwick for a month's location filming, each horse having two handlers, it doesn't come cheap.'

The follow-up series, 'Blackadder II', was done mostly in the studio, cost about a third as much, and, says Atkinson, was 'a lot funnier'.

'Blackadder II' was moved about 100 years on into the Elizabethan age. Edmund Blackadder was the great grandson of the weedy and thoroughly unlikeable hero of the original series. From there we went to the late eighteenth century with three hapless heroes plaguing the court of mad George III and finally to the First World War with Captain Edmund Blackadder, the last of his dastardly line, in the trenches.

Atkinson believes that as Blackadder moved through the ages his appeal widened and, for the first time, gave him an audience which stretched beyond the 35 age limit.

'By the time the third 'Blackadder' hit the screens a lot of middle-aged and elderly people were coming up to me and saying nice things. And the last one broke both the age and class barriers completely. There was enough rudeness for the young and intelligence for the over-fifties. The young always make up the most enthusiastic part of an audience but we were getting 15 million viewers for a 9.30 slot on television and that cannot be achieved through young people alone.

'I suppose my own maturity also meant that subconsciously I was widening my appeal into middle age and beyond.'

Killing off a highly successful TV series at just the right time before it becomes stale and boring can be difficult with both the public and TV bosses clamouring for more. I've often spoke at length to Ian La Frenais, the co-creator of 'Porridge' and 'Auf Wiedersehen Pet', about resisting the temptation to do one series too many and Atkinson has much the same thoughts on the subject.

'It's easier now because I've got greater confidence in my own judgement,' he told me. 'We did four series of 'Not The Nine O'Clock News' and left it at its peak and similarly we did four 'Blackadders'. By then you have achieved what you set out to achieve. Repeating the formula is not a creative challenge.'

So what is now? I spoke with Rowan on the phone back in May, the day he flew in from the Montreux Festival. He'd stayed only two days in Switzerland and left before the awards were announced. The previous year he had missed out with

'Blackadder' but, shortly after my call, he received another to say that he had swept the board as a madcap eccentric in the virtually silent 'Mr Bean', a one-off show he'd done for Thames Television. Atkinson had won the coveted Golden Rose of Montreux plus a Special Prize of the City of Montreux for the funniest programme and the Press Prize for the best programme entered by broadcasters.

And that meant we'd see a lot more of Mr Bean . . . and hopefully see Atkinson take his TV popularity onto the big screen. In his restless world that was to be his next challenge.

'Films are a great uncharted territory for me. There is a sharp line between TV and films and I need to breach that. But the British film industry seems to be very dark, dingy and violent at the moment. The only parts are the butler or an art gallery proprietor. What I'd like to make is an American film, something funny.

'It may be that I've got to create my own project, something tailor-made to my particular talents. Someone is already working full-time on such a possibility. But I wouldn't want to play the only big role. I would prefer to co-star with an established film star because it would make it easier to find the finance.'

Rowan may be out of the Cleese school of comics but he is full of admiration for the stand-up comedians.

'I think Les Dawson is very funny and Bob Monkhouse has a sharp wit. I also saw Bruce Forsyth warm up an audience and he was sparkling. Perhaps I admire them because they can do something I could never do. I can't be funny at the drop of a hat.'

That comes back to the Rowan Atkinson personality, of course. He's an intensely private man whose friends tend to be 'in the business' but not necessarily other performers. Often they are writers or directors. One of them, fellow-comedian Stephen Fry, was best man among only a handful of guests when he married stunning Sunetra Sastry in secret in New York in February, 1990. It was typical of him to shun publicity for such a highly personal event.

The fame and adulation rest uneasily on his slim shoulders, especially when he comes home to Tyneside.

'The funny thing generally about coming back,' he said

shortly after his early TV successes, 'is the recognition bit. It gives me a strange feeling. It's all right when it happens somewhere like Reading or Birmingham and you're being fussed over and asked for autographs a lot. But when it happens in places which you have known so well when you weren't known at all yourself, with places and people you thought didn't change at all, it begins to worry you.

'I'd always been able to come home to Newcastle and it was like it was, if you follow my meaning. Then suddenly it wasn't at all — people were stopping and staring in places I used to walk along every day of my life.'

The considerable changes which a city or area undergoes with the passage of time always produce a certain sadness in an exile whose memories remain locked steadfastly in childhood or adolescence. In the last decade and a half since Atkinson called Tyneside home many of his old haunts have disappeared.

'I arranged a rendezvous with a friend once and suggested meeting outside the Northumberland Arms in Northumberland Street, one of our old haunts. We turned up and it wasn't there. I was shocked to find a bit of Eldon Square shopping centre jutting out instead.

'My feelings whenever I come back are sad and nostalgic really. It's like going back to your first school — everything seems smaller than you remember it.

'For the first 17 years of my life I lived in Consett and we all know what's happened there in recent years with the steel-works closing down. Now it's a real eye-opener. The town's no longer thriving and all the shops I remember from my youth are selling anything they can get their hands on. The butcher's shop, for example, was selling Christmas cards as well. It sticks in my mind.'

The Newcastle city centre itself has changed, too, since his time at university.

'While I was there they always seemed to be building motorways and it was rather depressing. Each week they were slicing through a new bit and we had to keep walking along different routes. More and more tarmac appeared and suddenly we weren't allowed on the motorway at all, they were finished and opened. By then I'd left so I never got to know the motorway system or Eldon Square.'

The North East may have changed, but then so has Rowan Atkinson . . . from just another Geordie into a superstar who provides us with one of life's greatest pleasures. The feeling of laughter.